The Other Side of
Complicated Grief: Hope in
the Midst of Despair

The Other Side of Complicated Grief: Hope in the Midst of Despair

Rhonda O'Neill R.N.

ISBN: 0997800704
ISBN 13: 9780997800708
Library of Congress Control Number: 2016911456
Saudade Publishing, Wichita, KANSAS

For my daughters, Megan, Kathryn, and Maggie,
And my mother, Julie.
In memory of my son, Jordan, and my late-husband, Steve.
Thank you for teaching me everything
I need to know about Love,
Especially that Love never dies.

Acknowledgements

WRITING A BOOK about grief is a very personal endeavor and I had many reservations about sharing such private and devastating aspects of my life. I received encouragement and support from several of my loved ones. My biggest cheerleaders have been my daughters, my mother, my sister Kris, and my dear friend, and cousin, Kristi. Thanks to all of you for always encouraging me. My grandson, Ethan, holds a special place in my life and deserves a special thank you for always making my heart feel all fuzzy and warm. A thank you also goes out to my husband, Michael, for being a good sounding board when I needed feedback on challenging areas of the book.

My dear friends, Scott and Tammy Wagner, have provided a great deal of support, frequently asking, "How's the writing going?" Scott, who is an English Writing major, has on numerous occasions given me excellent feedback and encouragement. Thank you, Scott!

Dr. Katherine Shear, director of The Center for Complicated Grief, and her website, has been an exceptional source of information regarding the clinical facts of complicated grief and effective treatments that have been developed. Her unique and empathetic approach to those suffering with complicated grief has been quite refreshing. Her belief that, "Grief does not happen without great love," says it all.

My editor, Sarah Aschenbach, has been a joy to work with and has provided invaluable guidance in my writing, while also managing to maintain my writer's voice. Thank you for sharing your wisdom and giving your honest feedback, enabling me to clearly convey the message I wanted to send to my potential readers.

Lastly, thank you to my family for helping my children and me through our grieving process, especially during the early days when even getting out of bed was difficult for me. I am forever grateful to my parents, Julie and Bob; my three sisters, Michelle, Kristen, and Robyn; my brothers-in-law, Curtis, Roger, and Dustin; and my nine nieces and nephews. Your support and love, during the difficult years will always be remembered.

Table of Contents

My Message to fellow grievers

Out of suffering have emerged the strongest souls; the most massive characters are seared with scars.

—KAHLIL GIBRAN

Some things in life can't be fixed, they can only be carried.

—MEGAN DEVINE

IF YOU HAVE opened this book, I can only assume that you have lost someone you love, and that you are struggling to find your way through the despair of grief. Before I share my story, I first want to encourage you: Although right now it doesn't feel like it, you *can* learn to carry this pain and to live your life again. I also want you to know that you are not being punished or tested by life or by God. You haven't done anything to deserve the loss of your loved one or the suffering you are going through. Pain and change are unavoidable parts of this human existence.

If someone had told me ten years ago that I would be writing about grief, I wouldn't have believed it. I had struggled with many obstacles in my early adult life, and I didn't believe there was anything I couldn't handle. By the time I was thirty-eight, my life had fallen into place. I was happily remarried after struggling for years as a single parent of three. My husband and I had added a beautiful daughter to our large, blended family of seven children. My son, who'd had two kidney transplants, was healthy and thriving at the time. I was a nurse who now enjoyed being a stay-at-home mom. My life felt blessed. I was content and fulfilled. My family was happy and healthy. Life was perfect.

A lot can change in ten years.

2006 was the year my husband died in an airplane accident, five days after our daughter's second birthday.

I was unprepared for the anguish I experienced. I sank into a deep sense of hopelessness that engulfed every aspect of my life. After a year of barely surviving, I slowly began to repair my life and my family. I remained sad and in pain, but I was able find some joy again. I had survived, but I would never be the same.

I thought that the death of my late-husband was the worst thing that could ever happen to me...but I was wrong.

In 2008, my twenty-year-old son died of complications from kidney failure.

That time, my grief looked quite different as it morphed into complicated grief. I was caught off guard by the enormous expanse of raw and debilitating emotions that assailed me. My pain turned into anger, and my anger into resentment. I resented life, God—I resented everything and almost everyone. I was skeptical and bitter for several years, like an unlucky pawn in some elaborate cosmic game that, until then, I had been unaware that I was engaged in, and I was tired of playing the game.

My health began to fail me, and I experienced several life-threatening health crises. It seemed no part of my life was within my control. Every time that I began to heal from my losses or health problems, a new crisis erupted, setting my healing journey back several steps. I couldn't seem to catch my breath from the misfortunes that pummeled me.

The pendulum of my life rapidly swung from the peak of perfect happiness to its lowest point, where the pendulum appeared to be frozen within a nightmare I could not escape. Two of the people I loved most in the world were gone. My previously healthy body was no longer supporting me. I didn't know how to go on living the story of my life, as every page I turned to after the loss of my loved ones was blank. There were no instructions on how to get through the pain and no indication that I could ever find relief from the suffering. The very purpose that had driven my life seemed to have died right along with my lost loved ones. Suddenly, the girl who had been sure she had this life thing under control didn't have a clue how to move forward.

Everything in my life stopped making sense to me, and I was desperate for answers. At times, I felt I might lose my mind. I mean, how much could one person be expected to bear without breaking? Could God not see that I needed help? I didn't understand how any of it worked. Why is there so much suffering in the world? Is there any purpose to it? Why do people die who have so much to live for, while others who seem to have miserable, unwanted lives continue to live? What is the meaning of life when in the end we all just die? And where is God amidst all of this pain?

My unanswered questions about why these things had happened to me—about why things like this happened to *anyone*—pushed me to challenge all of my beliefs. A sense that there were answers out there waiting for me to discover propelled me, answers that could bring some relief and stability to my life again.

My eventual healing came through a search for philosophical, metaphysical, and spiritual answers to the greater meaning of life and death. While I can't say that I found concrete answers to all of my questions, I did find enough answers to help me discover my personal spiritual path. It is a path that helped me work through the acute anguish of grief, learn to live with loss, and find a way to choose life again.

This book is the one I wish I could have read when I was struggling in despair; it is my contribution to others who are searching to find their way.

The book has three sections. Section 1 is a memoir about my life, both the losses and the blessings. Section 2 is about complicated grief, and it contains practical and professional tools for healing your grief. Here, I also talk about the impact that our death-denying Western society has on grief. Section 3 addresses the spiritual and philosophical questions that arose after my late-husband and son died and the tools that helped me find my personal spiritual path, which was essential to repairing my broken heart.

I want to emphasize that I share my personal path with you not as an endorsement of what I believe your path should be, but as an example of the process I went through to find my way out of the misery of complicated grief. I know not everyone will resonate with what I have written, but I hope you can find some relief as you read about my experiences and discoveries. And I encourage you to search for questions and answers of your own. Seek out your own path. Discover what makes sense to you. Take from my book the sections that work for you and put aside the ones that do not. We each have a unique path to walk. You can find yours.

I would be a hypocrite if I led you to believe that once you've gotten to a place where you can live with some joy again, you'll never have moments of grief. The unavoidable and brutal truth is that you will never "get over" the loss of someone you loved so dearly. You will never be the same. Life will never be the same.

You will always miss them; a part of you left with them when they died.

This journey through grief is not for the weak of heart, but you have more courage than you think. You *can* learn to carry this pain. Overcoming the debilitating pain of complicated grief takes hard work. If you picked up this book, I believe it is because you are ready and determined to find a way to relieve some of the pain you are in.

Grief knocked me down for the count and took ten years of my life. Now, I am back up on my feet, and I want the next ten years to be different from the previous ten. I now make the active choice every day to do my best to find some joy in my life. Some days are harder than others, and it was a hell of a journey to get to the point where I am finally able to make a choice about how I am going to spend my day instead of allowing grief to make the choice for me. Honestly, there are still some days, or partial days, when I choose to stay in the pain. Some days, it is just too much work to get out of those painful emotions. I recognize that this is my choice, just as it is your choice to choose how you spend your days. My choices are fairly clear to me at this point: am I going to do my best to live each day, or am I going to surrender my day by living in memories and emotions? This doesn't mean that I will ever forget my lost loved one. Nor will you. That will never happen. Our loved ones will always be part of our hearts and our lives. But we can learn to carry the memories while still finding a way to live in the present moment.

Remember, the journey through grief is a matter of perspective. I know it feels like you can never make it out, but you can. Honor your pain and your loss and keep moving forward, one step at a time and one day at a time. Eventually your perspective on grief and life will change. That doesn't mean that it won't still be hard or that the pain will ever go away, but it does change; it can become bearable. You can learn to carry it.

Don't let grief take more of your life than it already has. Healing grief and learning to live without your loved one is the hardest thing you will ever do, but love and loss can learn to walk side by side into the future. By honoring your pain and your lost loved one, you can find a way to live again.

And, as you go forward, know that you are not alone.

Rhonda

PART 1

Losses and Blessings

CHAPTER 1

The Paradox within the Tapestry of Life

Mostly it is loss which teaches us the worth of things.

—Arthur Schopenhauer

We must not allow the clock and the calendar to blind us to the fact that each moment of life is a miracle and a mystery.

–H.G. Wells

This first section of the book is a memoir—and not only the misfortunes I've experienced in my life, but also the gifts, gifts that often I didn't appreciate until tragedy invaded my life and plucked my loved ones away before I was prepared to let them go. Upon reflection, I now metaphorically see life as the weaving of a multi-dimensional tapestry, the painful and undesirable experiences in life adding as much depth and meaning to the tapestry as the joyful. No matter how difficult they are, the dark threads are essential to highlight the light threads within the pattern. Fused together, the tragic and the sacred define the richness and durability of the finished tapestry, ultimately revealing the underlying and significant role that pain plays in life. We naively believe that suffering is something we can avoid or outrun, but as many of us have discovered, this type of pain is relentless, and there is no escaping it.

The intense anguish of grief can make you want to turn away from life. I did that for many years. Living with the pain and permanent loss of your loved ones makes it impossible to deny the transient nature of the world. With time, I have come to accept that, not only am I not promised tomorrow, neither are any of my remaining loved ones. Facing this reality has helped me arrive at a place where I can be grateful for the time I have with my loved ones today, seeing it for the blessing it is. If we look, we will find insights into life's mysteries in all of our experiences, both the good and the bad, both the desired and the undesired. Understanding this seeming paradox can help us endure the pain of grief. When we have gotten through the acute stages of pain, some aspect of that experience helps us engage more fully in life and embrace all its elements.

Some will tell you that grief makes you stronger. I don't know about you, but I never asked or wanted to be stronger. I only wanted my loved ones and my life back. I am not stronger because of my pain. I may be more resilient, but it came with a price. The pain of grief can break you. Not everyone makes it through to the other side. Many people have been destroyed mentally, physically, and emotionally from the death of someone they love. However, if you allow the ebb and flow of healing, you can learn to adapt to the pain. This gives you a more objective view of life and eventually allows you to be witness to both the beauty and the pain of this human experience. Such is the life-altering capacity of pain. It can destroy you; or, if you surrender to the inevitable tragedy of it all, pain can eventually forge you into a vessel that can embrace and experience life: the reality of its transience; all its agonizing and sacred offerings; extremes of love and loss, bliss and misery, hatred and passion, beauty and heartache, and health and illness. This is life in all its multi-faceted, exquisite, and astounding insanity and harmony.

You can be broken and still find a way to move on and find beauty in the midst of despair. There is an ancient Japanese tradition in which broken objects are mended by fusing the cracks together with gold. The Japanese believe that something that has suffered damage and has a history has only been made more unique and beautiful. This can be true for you, as well.

Many times we don't recognize the unique worth and durability that can be found within the scars of our mended wounds. While we would rather not have to be broken to find our resilience, the finished product has a beauty and value that cannot, and should not, be denied.

CHAPTER 2

Life and Love, Discovered and Lost

Your pain is the breaking of the shell that encloses your understanding.

—*KAHLIL GIBRAN*

YEARS AGO, I was one of those people who managed to breeze through life, the perpetual fly-by-the-seat-of–your-pants girl who always managed to land on her feet. Despite my acrobatic abilities, I still experienced a few troubles in my early adult life: caring for a chronically ill son who'd had a kidney transplant at the age of two and a second transplant at the age of fourteen; putting myself through nursing school while I had three children under the age of six; ending a dysfunctional marriage that involved infidelity and addiction; and then, struggling as a single parent and the primary support for three adolescent kids.

Although my life had more than its fair share of stress, I was meeting life's basic needs. I sincerely thought my life was good, and despite the occasional pit stops, I was always able to find those positive aspects. I loved my job as a pediatric intensive care nurse.

I had loving and supportive parents and three sisters who helped me and my children through the tough times.

Life as I knew it changed in January of 2002 when I met a man by the name of Steve O'Neill. When we met, I was a single parent of three children: Megan, fifteen; Jordan, thirteen; and Kathryn, twelve. Honestly, my time and finances had stretched about as far as they could, and I focused any free time I had on caring for my children. In the three years since my divorce, I had dated very little. In fact, by the time I met Steve, not one man had met my children. Steve quickly changed that. And here, I want you to keep in mind that my family was not the typical family. My thirteen-year-old son, Jordan, had significant health care needs.

Jordan had been born in February of 1988 with congenital ne-phrotic syndrome, a rare kidney disease. The doctors informed me that he wouldn't live past two years old without a kidney transplant. This kidney disease caused extreme fluid overload that eventually led to congestive heart failure and fluid collecting in his lungs. The disease also caused severe immunosuppression. Before his transplant, we averaged two weeks out of the month in the hospital, and he ended up in ICU and came close to death several times.

Finally, when Jordan was 23 months old, I was able to donate one of my kidneys to him. We traveled from Wichita to Kansas City for the surgery. At that time, he was the youngest child in the Midwest to receive a kidney transplant. After the transplant, Jordan had several major rejections, and we were in the hospital for a total of three months until his rejections were finally under control. Unfortunately, the acute rejections caused permanent damage to his transplanted kidney, and Jordan developed a condition called chronic rejection. At some point in the future, his kidney would fail, and Jordan would require another transplant.

Despite this unsettling prognosis, Jordan remained fairly healthy over the next eleven years. All three of my children thrived, despite the divorce, and they had minimal contact with their father. Although healthy, Jordan still required expensive anti-rejection medications and routine medical follow-up care, which was difficult on a single parent's budget. There were many months I wasn't sure I could cover all of our expenses, but we always seemed to make it through.

When Steve and I met through a mutual friend in 2002, we hit it off from our first date. We talked for hours, and it seemed like we had known one another forever. No one had ever made me laugh so much in my life. He made me feel like a kid again. And more than that, he was a credible guy, a petroleum engineer who had worked successfully in the field for seventeen years. Also a pilot, he was working as a regional sales manager for an international aircraft company. Oh, and he was also pretty darn handsome! Most important, he showed genuine interest in my children and me. He understood that dating me was a package deal and made that very clear. He knew I would not be with anyone who couldn't treat my children with love and respect.

Steve and I had dated for six weeks when Jordan's transplanted kidney went into an acute and complete rejection. Steve had been planning to go out of town that weekend for work and had invited me to go with him. I had been looking forward to spending that time with him, but instead, I prepared to make the three-hour drive to take Jordan up to Children's Mercy Hospital, where his specialists would care for him and start hemodialysis.

I'll never forget how I cried as I drove through the pouring rain to Kansas City, my sick son asleep in the back seat. How ironic could life be? I had finally met a wonderful man I thought I could have a future with, and Jordan had become dangerously ill with no relief in sight. What sane man would seriously consider taking on my life?

I soon received my answer. Steve cancelled his weekend trip and showed up the following day at the hospital. He stayed with us until Jordan's dismissal. Steve was by my side as the doctors talked with Jordan and me about what we should expect. We headed home with plans for Jordan to continue dialysis and be placed on the national kidney transplant list. Steve wanted to support all of us, and he became a regular fixture around our household.

In hindsight, I can see that Steve did what I did not allow anyone else in my adult life to do. Although I had gratefully received a lot of support from my family to help care for my kids, I still felt very alone, and I was under a lot of pressure to support my children, financially and emotionally. Steve immediately made it clear that he not only wanted to support me, he wanted to take care of me.

Now, don't get me wrong: I didn't need anyone to take care of me. I was an independent woman and had proven I could take care of myself and my children. With three small children at home, I had put myself through nursing school after Jordan's transplant because I knew I would have to support my children on my own one day. I had gone through hell and back to provide for my children and keep them healthy, and I was proud of what I had accomplished. But, honestly, I was exhausted. I had always been the strong and responsible one who cared for others, at my job and at home.

When Steve and I fell in love, he saw how overwhelmed I was. He wanted to take care of my children and me. Not only did I let him, I depended on his strength. I had always been the strong one, but when Steve offered me his reliable shoulder to lean on, this warrior mom put down her shield, took off her armor, and let herself be vulnerable. I felt more cared for and secure than at any other time in my life.

Steve and I went on to nurture our relationship as he helped me care for Jordan, who was on hemodialysis three days a week and not tolerating it well. The physicians had a hard time regulating his phosphorous and magnesium levels, and Jordan experienced extreme leg cramps that made it very painful to walk. He had to use crutches and sometimes a wheelchair to get around. Jordan was small for a thirteen-year-old; he weighed only about ninety pounds. When we were out doing something as a family, Steve picked Jordan up and carried him in his arms wherever we went, leaving the crutches and wheelchair behind. I'll never forget the smile on Jordan's face when Steve carried him. In so many ways, Steve worked his way into all of our hearts.

Jordan underwent his second kidney transplant in July of 2002 in Wichita. He received this kidney from his Aunt Michelle, one of my three sisters. During the surgery, one of the biggest aviation conferences of the year was happening in Wisconsin, and Steve was unable to get out of working there. The morning of the surgery, he called me every hour for an update. Finally, at noon, Steve told his boss he couldn't take it anymore, that he had to be with Jordan and my family at the hospital. He flew himself back to Wichita, along the way making an emergency landing because of low oil pressure. He had the airplane fixed and headed back out on his way. Arriving at the hospital around eleven p.m., he pulled up a second recliner next to mine at Jordan's bedside in the SICU, where he remained at our sides.

Jordan underwent a series of major rejections over the next two months but, with the help of very serious intravenous anti-rejection treatments, his body eventually accepted the transplanted kidney. Once again, however, we were told that this transplanted kidney had sustained permanent damage, causing chronic rejection. At some point in the unknown future, it, too, would fail.

Throughout his life, Jordan was always such a trooper. He never wanted anyone to feel sorry for him. But as his mother, I found it very hard to see him go through so much. I didn't want him ever to feel that he was in this fight alone. Throughout the years, even when he was a teenager, I always slept in a recliner at his bedside when he was in the hospital. I'll never forget what he said to me after his second transplant, when he was enduring all the misery of the rejection treatments and central line placements and biopsies. He took my hand and looked me in the eyes. "Mom, " he said, "you're the only one who understands what I go through. Thank you for being here." The truth is, there was nothing more important to me, than being by my son's side as he went through his struggles. We were in this fight together.

Every pain he endured was imprinted on my heart. I had created a name for this when I worked as a nurse and witnessed other mothers showing this same maternal drive to protect their children. I called it Mama Bear Syndrome. To an outsider, the mom might seem irrational and impossible to please. However, for the mother of a chronically ill child, there is only so much pain you can bear to see your child undergo. There is only so much suffering you are willing to see them endure before your protective instinct takes over and you demand that someone, anyone, take your child's pain away. Heaven help the nurse or doctor who makes a mistake on your child or doesn't care for them according to your high standards. Not a pretty picture. Needless to say, I developed a Mama Bear reputation in the hospital. By the time of Jordan's dismissal, the hospital staff was just as glad to see us go home as we were to be going.

Steve proposed to me five months after Jordan's transplant, and we married in January of 2003 in Costa Rica. As we merged our two households and families, our life was a whirlwind. Steve brought three adolescent children of his own into our marriage. Between the two of us, we had six teenagers, ages eleven through sixteen. In many ways, we were a modern-day Brady Bunch—but with a few additional issues. Not surprisingly, a couple of the kids were not on board with blending our families and put up some resistance. Throw into the mix the hormones of teenagers, and we had some challenges on our hands. However, the strong love Steve and I shared always got us through the tough times. My children blossomed under Steve's fatherly guidance and love. Steve and I were very happy despite the road bumps, and our relationship flourished.

Six months later we discovered that our family would be getting larger and we would be adding our own child to the mix. My oldest daughter was eighteen by then, so I was a little shocked, but I was also thrilled to be expecting. Because I was thirty-six, my pregnancy was considered high risk and I was monitored closely. The pregnancy advanced without problems until my eighth month, when I had an episode in which I passed out. I was still working full time, so I just thought I was overdoing things. The next day at my routine OB appointment, they sent me to the hospital for tests. There, we discovered that I'd had a pulmonary embolism (PE) from a 17 cm blood clot found in my right thigh. Several hours after admission, I threw my second PE. As I was passing out and hearing my heart rate dropping on the monitor, my field of vision narrowed to a small circle. I saw the nurse's feet as she ran into the room. Even more concerning, I could hear the baby's heart rate drop as everything went black.

The baby and I made it through the second PE, and I was started on a heparin IV drip to dissolve the clot, which the doctors said would take months. The risk of another PE was high, and with each PE, my risk of survival continued to drop. During this time, it seemed to me that the hospital staff was tiptoeing around me. No one could tell me what the plan was if I were to have another PE.

I was uncomfortable being on the receiving end of medicine and its uncertainty. I had been a pediatric intensive care nurse and trauma-certified for more than a decade, and I wanted confirmation that both my baby's and my life were in capable hands. I insisted on being informed of what the plan was if I threw another PE. The doctors had withheld the information from me because they didn't want to worry me. Reluctantly, then, they informed me that the trauma team was on call and prepared to crack my chest open to perform an emergency pulmonary endarterectomy to clear the PE. Simultaneously, the OB would do an emergency C-section to save the baby. The doctors were afraid that this information would further stress me, but once I knew there was a plan in place to improve the miniscule odds of our survival, I found some peace of mind. Truthfully, my primary concern was my baby's survival; I didn't think there was much chance that I would survive this situation.

As we were forced to face the possibility that I would die, Steve and I discussed what would happen to my three children. Steve insisted that he be allowed to adopt Megan, Jordan, and Kathryn and raise them as his own. Their biological father was not involved in their lives at that point, so we talked with the kids about it. They were concerned and upset about the possibility of my death, but knowing that Steve would take care of them if something happened brought them some comfort, I think. It certainly brought me great peace of mind.

During this time, my mother and three sisters began praying to a deceased Italian woman who was up for sainthood in the Catholic Church, Gianna Beretta Molla. A physician who put her life at risk in the 1950s when she was diagnosed with a cancerous tumor during her fourth pregnancy. She refused treatment for the cancer because it would harm her unborn child. Months later, she delivered a healthy baby girl, but Gianna died a few weeks after the birth of her daughter due to complications from the cancer. The Church canonized her in 2005, in part because she had sacrificed her life for her child's. Prayer was a confusing subject for me, as I will discuss in a later chapter, but desperate for my baby and me to survive, I was grateful to receive any additional help that Gianna might send to us.

Eleven days after my family had begun praying to Gianna Beretta Molla, the sonographers were not able to find the 17 cm blood clot. It didn't appear that it had migrated, either; instead, it seemed to have disappeared. It was a mystery. The physicians had no medical explanation, as a clot of that size typically took three or four months to dissolve. I don't understand how miracles work, why some people receive them when other people don't, but I know something happened to make that blood clot disappear. I accepted the gift thankfully, and I felt fortunate to be alive.

Two weeks later, on March 23, 2004, I delivered a beautiful, healthy baby girl. We named her Margaret Gianna and called her Maggie. Maggie brought our blended family together as never before, and Steve and I were thrilled to have a living reminder of our love. We left the hospital feeling blessed that both Maggie and I had made it through the hospitalization with very few long-term complications. The physicians diagnosed me with a coagulation disorder called Protein S deficiency. I was put on the blood thinner Coumadin, which I remained on for five years, and a coagulation filter was placed in my inferior vena cava. The filter would prevent any blood clots that might develop in my lower extremities from going to my heart, lungs, or brain. While this was all a bit over-whelming, I was extremely thankful to be alive.

Life was quite busy with a little one and six teenagers under the roof, but our family thrived during this time. Steve was moving up the sales ladder at the aircraft company; he had received a promo-tion to regional sales manager of western North America, which increased his travel time. He averaged one to two weeks out of town every month, which he found hard. He missed the family and always did his best to get back home as quickly as possible. When he was out of town, we followed a routine. He called multiple times during the day, and when he was flying, he always called me before takeoff and again when he landed to let me know everything was okay.

By Maggie's first birthday, our two oldest daughters were go-ing to college and we had four teenagers in high school. Life was extremely busy. With Steve out of town so much, we decided it would be best if I quit my job and stayed home to care for Maggie and manage the household. I was happy and ready to stay at home. I had missed a lot of my older children's youth due to work and wanted to be there for them during their teenage years. I also wanted to spend time with Maggie. She was such a happy baby and was growing up fast. Maggie was the missing puzzle piece that our blended family needed to be complete. Everyone adored her, especially her daddy.

In May of 2005, we were caught off guard again when I had a mole removed on my upper right thigh and was diagnosed with amelanotic melanoma, which was rare. I was fortunate that the specialists were able to remove it with two surgeries, and I didn't re-quire chemotherapy or radiation. They told me I was very lucky I'd come in, because the melanoma was close to the depth at which it starts to metastasize. For the rest of my life, I would require routine monitoring of my skin because of the high risk for additional skin cancers. Over the next nine years, eleven basal cell and squamous cell carcinomas were removed from my body.

We felt relieved that we had found the melanoma early, but we were concerned about future complications that might arise from my rapidly multiplying medical problems. Our focus was on my health. Nowhere on our radar was the possibility that something might happen to Steve.

By the third year of our marriage, our family life was settled and tranquil. During that year, we created many happy family memories. Steve and I worked very hard to make sure each child in our family knew how loved he or she was and that each felt a vital part of the family. The trust and love among us solidified, and we finally became a family in every sense of the word.

Maggie's second birthday came on March 23rd of 2006. Steve was scheduled to leave on a work trip later that afternoon, so we kept her birthday celebration small. Steve and I had birthday cupcakes with Maggie, who looked adorable in pigtails. We sang "Happy Birthday" to her while she blew out her two candles. I have a picture of this moment: the look of adoration and love on Steve's face as he was singing to Maggie is priceless. Later, Maggie "helped" Steve assemble her present, a new Disney Princess tricycle.

After playing with Maggie, Steve and I began our customary process of preparing for his trip. We worked together to pack his bags just as we had done dozens of times over the last three years of our marriage. I had no idea that it was the last time we would experience this domestic routine together. He was flying a plane out to California to demonstrate it to potential buyers and anticipated being gone for around two weeks. An avid cyclist, he took his road bike with him on long trips so he could exercise and enjoy the scenery wherever he traveled.

Maggie and I had to pick up one of the older kids, so we said our goodbyes as we were leaving the house. Steve had a big hug and kiss for both Maggie and me. I was backing my car out of the garage when Steve came out the back door into the garage, carrying his bike to his SUV, a big smile on his face. He blew another kiss to both of us. I drove away, unaware that it was the last time I would ever see him. The memory of him smiling as he held his bike will be forever imbedded in my mind. I can see it as clearly as if it had been yesterday.

The next five days went by routinely, Steve calling to check on us multiple times a day, as always. When the afternoon of the 28th rolled around, Steve and I had already talked several times. He and a colleague had finished a demo and planned to head out for their next destination around five p.m. my time. They would be in the air for about an hour, and he would call me when he landed.

I got distracted by some teenage drama that Jordan was having, and the next time I looked at the clock, it was after seven p.m. I was surprised that Steve hadn't yet called, so I called him. The call went directly to his voicemail. I assumed that he was still in the air and that we'd miscommunicated about the time of his landing. I went back to dealing with the drama and completing our family's evening routine.

When I still hadn't heard from him by nine p.m., I was somewhat concerned. Once again, though, I assumed that he was fine or that something was wrong with his phone.

I look back now and can't believe I wasn't more worried. The thought of something drastic happening to Steve was not even a remote possibility in my mind. I called and left another message. It went straight to voicemail again. It seems unbelievable to me now, but I was so tired that I fell asleep while putting Maggie to bed. I kept my phone beside me so I wouldn't miss Steve's call.

A little after eleven p.m., the phone rang. I answered groggily, expecting to hear Steve's voice. But it wasn't Steve. It was Steve's boss. He said he was at my front door. Completely confused, I went to the front door with no idea that life as I knew it was about to come to a brutal, abrupt stop.

Steve's plane had disappeared from radar during bad weather in the mountains of San Bernardino. The aircraft company would fly my family and me out to California to await information about the search for survivors, which was already underway. All I can remember about this time is that I constantly felt I was going to throw up and that everything was surreal. I just couldn't believe it was happening.

I flew out to California on a private jet with my son, my parents, and several of Steve's brothers, one of whom had brought his hiking boots in case he could help with the rescue efforts. In the end, we just waited. We were in shock, even at that early point, but we were certain that he would be found alive. Death was not a possibility. Not for Steve.

On the second day, we received the news that neither Steve nor his colleague had survived the crash. After that, everything is a blur. I do remember noticing upon arriving back home that, within the last two days, all of our tulips had bloomed. It struck me as ironic and wrong that something so beautiful could be waiting for me at home when my heart, the very essence of me, was shattered.

Our wedding in 2003

Family Christmas 2005
Jordan, Megan, Kathryn, Me, Steve and Maggie

Steve reading to Maggie, 2006

Steve doing what he loved, flying.

CHAPTER 3

Descent into the Fog

The timing of death, like the ending of a story, gives a changed meaning to what preceded it.

—MARY CATHERINE BATESON

WHEN STEVE DIED, a bright source of light disappeared from my life, leaving me in a gray, weightless suspension that made me feel almost inanimate. It was the first time that I had experienced deep and unrelenting loneliness. Steve had been a constant source of love for me, a love that I equated to life itself. As sad and pathetic as it sounds, I didn't recognize myself without him by my side. The inner strength I had always prided myself on was nowhere to be found.

The following months were difficult for all of us. We had lost the head of our family, our compass. Maggie didn't understand where Daddy had gone or why Mommy was always so sad. I tried to be enough for everyone—for my children and stepchildren, but there just wasn't enough of me to go around. I didn't realize the long-term impact my grieving would have on my children. I wish I could have sheltered them better from the confusion and pain.

Looking back, I realize that I had a hard time seeing beyond my own pain to recognize the warning signs that my teenagers were showing me. Not only had my kids lost the man they considered their father, but they also had lost their mom to grief. I was attempting to help by regularly taking all of the kids to grief therapy, but it just wasn't enough. By the time I understood the turmoil, shock, and consequent self-destruction my teenagers were going through, it was too late to stop the landslide.

At sixteen, Kathryn, who had always been a model child, didn't know how to deal with her anguish. She started hanging around kids who were trouble. Meanwhile, I was struggling just to make it through the day, and honestly, taking care of Maggie was about as much as I could handle. I didn't notice the changes that were happening in Kathryn's life until I was unable to reverse the path she seemed determined to take. She became addicted to drugs and alcohol by the time she was seventeen and was in and out of multiple rehabs over the next eight years.

Jordan, too, was struggling and getting himself into trouble. He made several bad choices that had serious consequences, not only for him, but for all of us. The biggest consequence involved his kidney. Although I was providing him his anti-rejection medications, I was unaware that he wasn't taking them as required to keep his kidney healthy. Within a matter of months after Steve's death, Jordan rejected his second transplant and had to start hemodialysis again.

My world and family were coming apart at the seams, and I couldn't find the energy or the strength to put them back together. Regretfully, I was lost in my own world of grief, and I wasn't able to lead my older children out of their despair, which had turned into self-destruction. I look back now and wish I could have found the strength to do what needed to be done. But it just wasn't there. Steve's death and our inability to cope with it seemed to have changed the very fabric of my children's futures.

During this time, I did all that I could to protect two-year-old Maggie from the chaos that surrounded us. I regret that I became frustrated with my teenage kids for the poor choices they were making. How could they add more turmoil to our lives when we were already going through so much struggle? I understand now that this was the only way they knew how to deal with, and express, their heartache.

CHAPTER 4

A Mother's Love and Regrets

Never regret anything you have done with a sincere affection; nothing is lost that is born of the heart.

—BASIL RATHBONE

JORDAN REMAINED ON hemodialysis for two years. His body never adjusted to it. He had ongoing problems with his fistula and required frequent surgeries and procedures to keep it operable. Jordan was a poor candidate for a third transplant because of the rejections his body had gone through during his first two transplants, which had left antibodies standing at attention on behalf of his immune system, ready to attack any new foreign organ or substance introduced into his body. His odds of a third successful transplant were miniscule. Jordan also vividly remembered what he had gone through after the rejection of his second transplant. He was miserable on dialysis, but he wasn't willing to go through the torment of another transplant and possible rejection again.

As a nurse I knew that, without a kidney transplant, someone on dialysis has an average life expectancy of ten years. There seemed to be no solution in sight for Jordan, especially considering the suffering and complications he was experiencing on dialysis. Despite knowing this, I was still caught off guard when he sat me down for a talk in June of 2008.

Jordan wanted to stop dialysis. I knew that death would occur within one to two weeks without it, so my first reaction was shock and panic. I told him that stopping dialysis wasn't an option. But when I took a moment to actually look into his eyes, where I saw weariness and a desperation for understanding, I was forced to listen to what he had to say.

Jordan told me that he had been contemplating his options for a while. He had considered committing suicide because he wanted the pain to stop. But, he didn't want to put his family through the emotional pain of a suicide. He was tired of being cut on and prodded and poked. He was tired of feeling sick all the time with no relief in sight. He wanted it all to stop.

I felt like a terrible mother because I hadn't realized the depth of his physical and emotional anguish. Immediately, I called the nephrologist who had cared for him since he was five weeks old. We considered her a second mother to Jordan. She wanted the best for him. She had the same response to Jordan's request that I'd had: we couldn't allow him to do it. We agreed that he needed to be seen by a professional who could evaluate his emotional and psychological state.

I had taken Jordan to a child psychologist multiple times throughout his life, trying to help him deal with the stresses of his illness. After his request to stop dialysis, we made a trip back to him for help. The psychologist's specialty was helping children deal with their childhood illnesses, and he had gotten to know Jordan very well over the years.

Jordan talked with him at length about wanting to stop dialysis. His psychologist concluded that Jordan was of sound mind and was making a mature and informed decision about his life; Jordan's plea was not a search for attention. He was twenty years old, an adult, and he no longer wanted to live with either the emotional or physical pain of what had become of his life. His psychologist suggested that we honor Jordan's wishes.

I couldn't accept the psychologist's advice. I was desperate to change Jordan's mind. My daughters Megan, Kathryn, and I dropped everything to take Jordan on a road trip to Colorado, where we could talk with him and make sure he knew how important he was to all of us. Because of his dialysis schedule, we couldn't be gone long. We had three days to get him to change his mind.

We made many wonderful memories during those three days in Colorado. Since Jordan and I both struggled with insomnia, the two of us got up in the pre-dawn hours and headed out together. We drove towards the mountains and stopped to watch the sun rise above the summit. We were in awe of its majestic splendor. In a way, it seemed that these sunrises were meant specifically for us. I can't explain the serenity and sense of connection they granted us. I cherished this time with him.

We had deep conversations about Jordan's desire to end his life and about all the pain he had endured. In fact, he was in physical pain during the trip. We couldn't ignore what he was going through. Every day for him was a physical and emotional struggle. As his mother, I could see that my need for him to continue dialysis when there was no relief in sight was a selfish need. Jordan had valiantly fought his battles, and he was done with the fight. All he wanted were our blessings and support so that he could move on.

As we were driving home, Megan, Kathryn, and I came to a unanimous conclusion: Jordan was sincere in his desire to stop dialysis. We could no longer ignore his suffering. We had no doubt that he knew how much we loved him, and we would not stand in his way. We would support him in his decision to die and give him the love and dignity he deserved.

I am still astounded by the great courage and love it took for Jordan to make this decision. Instead of focusing on himself and his own fears, he worried about how his death would affect his mother, sisters, and grandmother. He did everything possible to make sure we were okay. I believe that if we had told him we didn't want him to stop dialysis, he would have continued his misery just for us.

Back home, we made the heartbreaking plans for Jordan to stop dialysis and go into in-patient hospice. We talked him into waiting until mid-September so we could spend more time with him. We all dreaded the coming of September and tried to ignore how rapidly it was approaching. We were also preparing a life celebration for Jordan, and we were looking forward to spending uninterrupted time as a family on another trip to Colorado.

Jordan decided to live the last two months of his life with my mother, his Grandma Julie. He had a very close relationship with her and wanted to spend that time with her. My mother was as heartbroken as the rest of us, but having witnessed his suffering for years, she wanted to love and support him through his decision. She brought him much comfort and joy in his last days.

Jordan used a small motorcycle to get around, mostly to go to dialysis and visit his friends. It was a Friday afternoon. I was preparing for the celebration, which was the next day. Dozens of close family and friends were coming over, and then on Monday, we would leave on our vacation. A few days after our return, Jordan was scheduled to go into hospice.

That Friday afternoon, I received a phone call that brought me to my knees. On the other end of the line was a police officer telling me Jordan's motorcycle was hit by a car. He was being taken by ambulance to a local hospital.

Nowhere in the vast potentials that the future might hold had I considered even a remote possibility that my son would be involved in an accident while we were planning his death. I wondered how this could be happening. Would the irony ever end? We had a lot of living planned for the next two weeks; we had a life celebration and a vacation to share with him. We needed more time. I wasn't in any way prepared to lose him in an accident.

When I arrived at the ER, I was relieved to find Jordan conscious and thankful that he did not seem to have any life-threatening injuries. He was experiencing significant pain from the extensive contusions he had sustained from the impact of the car. The ER staff was just as flabbergasted as I was that this could happen to someone about to go into hospice in a matter of weeks. They wanted to admit him because they were worried that the muscle damage he had sustained from the contusions could cause complications with his electrolyte levels and his cardiac function, and they also wanted to help control his pain.

Jordan insisted he didn't want to be hospitalized. He wanted to be home to enjoy his celebration and prepare for our vacation. The hospital staff and I reluctantly agreed, and we took him home, worried about how he would do. He was prescribed oral narcotics, but they didn't seem to be making much of a dent in his pain. But, as always, Jordan was a trooper and complained very little about what he was going through.

On Saturday afternoon, all of Jordan's family and friends rallied around him for his life celebration. We shared memories and stories amongst family and Jordan's friends. A photographer documented the bittersweet mixture of grief and love we were experiencing. These pictures are some of my most valued possessions.

Jordan was doing his best to enjoy the gathering, but his pain had become difficult to manage. Even walking was hard for him due to his muscle pain. I wanted to take him back to the hospital, but he insisted that he didn't want to go.

Later that night, along with the unrelenting pain, Jordan started having persistent vomiting. I insisted that he go back to the hospital; this time, he was in so much pain that he didn't resist. Test results showed that Jordan had severe rhabdomyolysis, which is a breakdown of muscle tissue that releases protein into the bloodstream, causing dehydration and electrolyte disorders. His serum potassium level was critically high at 9mg/dl, which put him at high risk for cardiac dysfunction. The doctors would have to work rapidly to try to reverse the damage. As they discussed their plans for treatment, Jordan stopped us all in our tracks. He didn't want treatment. He wanted to go into hospice, right then.

My heart dropped to the floor. I struggled with his decision. I wasn't ready to go there yet, and I tried one last time to change Jordan's mind. We were fortunate to have a physician's assistant named Joe, who spent a lot of time talking with Jordan and me about all the possibilities. Joe helped me hear what Jordan was trying to tell me. He had no more fight to give; he was done, and it was time.

Scottish poet Robert Burns said something about the best-laid plans often going awry. I had been preparing for my son to die as planned in September, not two weeks earlier in August. I find it interesting now that two weeks made such a difference to me, but they did. I can see now that, because of the plan, I had felt some modicum of control over the way my son would leave this earth, and so I was unprepared emotionally for the change. Jordan was only being logical. Why should he let the doctors put him through all those life-saving measures just so he could go into hospice two weeks later? As his mother, I was struggling with the path we were being forced to take, regardless of the logic. An emotion arose that was new to me: bitterness. Bitterness breached the surface of my awareness for the first time. I was finally understanding that life was indeed a cynical bitch, and I was infuriated.

Jordan spent three days in hospice. Throughout those days, we were at his side, determined that he would leave this earth surrounded by peace and knowing that he was loved. On the second day, Jordan and I were alone. Looking in my eyes, he told me that he was afraid. I told him he was going to be all right, that Steve would be there to help him. I deeply regret that I didn't encourage him to share more of his fears. Of course, he was scared. I was scared, and I wasn't the one dying. I wish I had been more prepared with words of comfort to present him. Although I'd had months to prepare for that day, I still wasn't comfortable with the conversation, or for that matter, with my son dying.

Jordan was comatose during his last twenty-four hours. It was excruciating to watch his body struggle through the process of death. Why couldn't anything be easy for him? As a nurse, I knew that Jordan was close to death by the end of the third day when he began having agonal breathing. As his breathing slowed and I watched him struggle to take each one, I could feel myself holding my own breath. Suddenly, he took a very large inhalation, almost a gasp, and then as he exhaled for the last time, he suddenly opened his eyes and looked directly into my eyes.

At that exact moment, I "felt" his spirit leave through his eyes and pass through my body. The sensation was similar to a concentrated gust of air traveling through me. I did not experience this sensation through my five senses, and it is difficult to describe with words. I believe that my spirit recognized Jordan's spirit as it left his body and that this was my son's parting gift to me.

I cried out his name and began to cry. No one else in the room realized what had happened until I yelled. Jordan had taken his last breath. His spirit had left his body.

What we witnessed for several hours after Jordan's death brought wonder and awe to our hearts. Jordan's body became so luminous that it looked almost flawless. Never in his life had we seen him look so radiant. In my nursing career, I had viewed many deceased bodies and had never witnessed anything like this. It was as if he wanted us to know that he was finally released from his agony and was experiencing bliss. We wondered if we were witnessing something of a miraculous nature. We understood the message he was sending to us, that he was fine and finally at peace. We knew that Jordan had left this physical existence knowing he was loved, and he was sending that love back to us from the spiritual realm. With joy in our hearts, we left the hospice unit to plan his funeral, which would be a positive celebration of his life.

I would be misleading you if I led you to believe that, because Jordan's death was planned and because I experienced these joyful and mystical moments, I was somehow relieved of some of my grieving. About a month after the funeral, unfortunately, I had forgotten all about the beautiful, spiritual moments surrounding Jordan's death. I began to focus on the loss of my child and was pulled back into an even deeper grief than I had experienced after Steve died. This time, the grief looked a little different.

I was sad and lonely after Steve died. I yearned for my life with him. After Jordan's death, I was angry and bitter and disillusioned with life. I became convinced that life was cruel and unjust, and I thought it very possible that God—if he even existed—was an asshole (yes, insert lightning bolt here). I came to believe that you had to fight against life with every ounce of strength you possess just to keep yourself and your family healthy and alive. And yet, as my own life showed, regardless of the quality of your defense, often you still experience defeat. I felt compelled to take up my warrior's persona again, the one I had worn as a single parent, complete with armor, shield, and sword. I felt I had to be on constant guard to control the circumstances in life. If God couldn't protect my family, then I was required to take on that job. I became hypervigilant about controlling my environment, which, as you can imagine, didn't go so well. Life had several more difficult lessons for me before I learned that control is just an illusion.

I questioned all the decisions I had made as Jordan's mother. Maybe I shouldn't have made him go through both transplants—look at all the suffering they had caused—and still he had died. Why had I agreed to let him stop dialysis? What kind of mother allows her child to, basically, commit suicide? No one else could have been harder on me than I was on myself.

I let myself slip further and further away from the reality of the circumstances that surrounded Jordan's life and death. I became consumed with grief and guilt. My emotions alternated between deep despair and anger at life and God, and it ate through my soul like a cancer. During this time, my emotional grief and anger were so powerful that they started turning into physical illness. I was making myself sick, but I wasn't aware enough to see the connection between my emotional state and how it was affecting my physical health.

By the one-year anniversary of Jordan's death, I was thoroughly miserable. My guilt was stifling. I was certain I was a horrible mother. My insomnia was worse than ever, and as I woke up very early the morning of that anniversary, I went over and over the negative aspects of how Jordan's life ended and how I should have done more to protect him. I began to feel claustrophobic and overwhelmed by all of my emotions. I had to get out of the house. I went to buy groceries at Walmart at five a.m. No one was in the store other than the employees. When I went to the cash register, a man walked up behind me. When I looked and realized that the man was Joe, the physician's assistant who had taken care of Jordan in the hospital, I froze and stared at him in disbelief.

Joe and I had an hour-long conversation about Jordan. Joe said he had never seen a patient who was so certain of what he wanted. Jordan had left Joe with no doubt that he wanted to go into hospice. He was ready for his physical life and the pain associated with it to be over. Joe had been very touched by caring for Jordan and had thought of him often over the past year.

I have no doubt that my son had somehow managed to arrange for Joe and me to meet in the store early that morning. I could feel Jordan watching over us as Joe reminded me of Jordan's wishes. Jordan was telling me to stop beating up on myself, and I heard his message. I still had a difficult path of grief before me, but this moment in my spiritual journey forced me to find a way to develop the tools to move on from the anguish of guilt.

While I was eventually able to resolve most of the guilt and regret, the extreme emotions I went through after Jordan died took a serious toll on my physical health. My emotions had been so intense that, like lined up dominoes, aspects of my physical health came tumbling down right behind my emotions.

I began having extreme autoimmune symptoms and was bedridden for a matter of months after Jordan died. I never fully recovered my health after his death. Unfortunately, I continued to experience a myriad of illnesses that further complicated the healing of my grief.

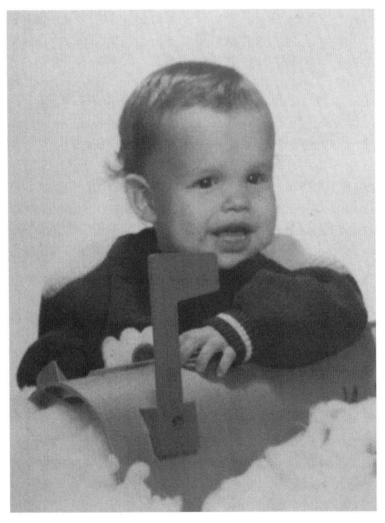

Jordan six months before his first transplant, 1991

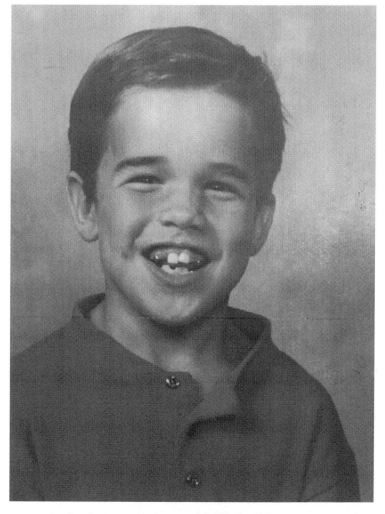

Jordan at seven years old. His healthy years.

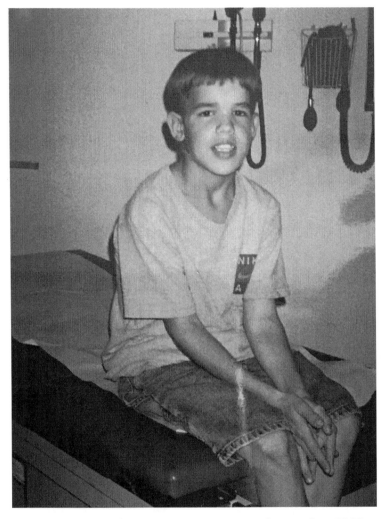

Jordan at thirteen, a year before his second transplant 2002

Jordan at 20 years old. Six days before he died.
Surrounded by Kathryn, Megan, Maggie and Me.

CHAPTER 5

The Physical Toll of Unresolved Complicated Grief

*You may not control all the events that happen to you, but
you can decide not to be reduced by them.*

—MAYA ANGELOU

AFTER YOU READ the upcoming section on complicated grief, if you believe you might have complicated grief, please take it seriously. This is the most important message I hope to get across. Complicated, untreated grief and the stress it creates in your body can make you sick. In fact, it can put your life at risk.

In May of 2010, a little less than two years after Jordan died, I was diagnosed with a basilar artery aneurysm (brain aneurysm). Of course, if I was going to have a brain aneurysm, it had to be the worst type. It was deep inside my brain, close to the brainstem. Only a handful of neurosurgeons in the country specialized in surgically repairing this type of aneurysm. As a nurse, I knew that a ruptured basilar artery aneurysm has a 66 percent mortality rate, and of the 34 percent who survive, half of them have serious, long-term neurological problems. Sometimes being a nurse really sucks when you are seriously ill. You know just how screwed you really are.

You might wonder how I felt upon learning that I had a ticking time bomb deep in my brain. My first thought was of Maggie, who was only six years old. How would she survive if she lost her mother two years after losing her brother and four years after losing her father? Three deaths in four years was too much to ask of someone so young, and she would be lost without me. It was just too much to think of Maggie and my older girls and my precious grandson (Megan now had a two-year-old son named Ethan) going through the rest of their lives without my guidance and support. I was determined to survive and not be another casualty that my family would have to endure.

I traveled to Chicago for a successful endovascular repair of the aneurysm. I will always be grateful for the excellent medical team that cared for me from Wichita to Chicago. I recovered physically within a week of the procedure. However, my emotional recovery and my family's took a bit longer.

Within the next two years, my medical team found another aneurysm, this time in my splenic artery. It is rare to have both a cerebral and a thoracic aneurysm. Lucky me. Then, masses started growing on my thyroid from the vast amounts of radiation I'd absorbed over the past ten years. I also averaged two new skin cancers requiring surgical removal every year. No matter how hard I tried, I could not seem to outrun these physical problems. The combined stresses of my traumatic confrontation with mortality due to these illnesses and a slide back into complicated grief took its toll. My autoimmune symptoms had flared up, off and on, over the years. During stressful events (a holiday or anniversary could land me in bed for days to weeks), my body exhibited flu-like symptoms, with fatigue and severe joint and muscle pain. I had been to numerous autoimmune, endocrine, hematology, and internal medicine specialists over the years, trying to figure out what was wrong with me. No one could give me a diagnosis.

All of it overwhelmed me and I felt that no one understood what I was going through with my physical decline and my emotional pain. In hindsight, I don't think even I realized that my suffering was connected directly to the grief of losing my husband and son. It had been years since they died. It just didn't occur to me that grief could have such a long-lasting impact.

I now know that all these symptoms—emotional, physical, and mental—were related to the unresolved and prolonged grief I was still experiencing.

When I was finally diagnosed with complicated grief in 2013, I had never heard the term. At the time, knowing this didn't really change anything for me. I wasn't concerned with whether what I was experiencing had a name because my doctor was not aware of any therapies that I wasn't already doing that could help complicated grief. I was miserable—that was all I knew. I was struggling to make it through the basics of day-to-day life. Eventually, I was diagnosed with and treated for MDD (major depressive disorder, which commonly occurs in unresolved and untreated complicated grief). Treatment for MDD didn't change my symptoms. I continued to struggle. Taking care of my young daughter was about all I could manage to do. In fact, if I hadn't had her to care for, some days I wouldn't have had the will to even get out of bed.

I was physically, mentally, and emotionally exhausted, and there were days I felt no hope that I would ever feel "normal" again. I could vaguely recall what it felt like to be happy and energetic, and I longed to feel that way again; I wanted to move on with life, but I couldn't seem to get the momentum. Each laborious step I took out of my grief didn't last long, as new life stressors and problems with my physical health seemed to trigger the grief and drag me backwards again so that I lost any ground I had previously gained.

I experienced the most disabling autoimmune flare up ever in January of this year (2016), after dealing with a stressful family event, and I have spent the majority of the last five months in bed with significant pain and exhaustion. As I write this, I am preparing to go to the Mayo Clinic for evaluation of an undifferentiated connective tissue autoimmune disorder and possible scleroderma.

After five days of seeing specialists and having tests at the Mayo Clinic, it was determined that I had the beginnings of the autoimmune disease, but the majority of my symptoms were from fibromyalgia, which the specialists believe was triggered by the grief and stress that I've endured over the last decade. Not only has grief taken years of my life, it is now also affecting my health and my future.

I can recognize now that some of these physical consequences might not have occurred if I had been properly treated for my complicated grief. The years of unresolved anguish and emotional distress caused many of my health complications.

Unresolved grief can make you sick.

While I realize you aren't expecting an anatomy and physiology tutorial on how stress affects the body, I think it is important to keep in mind that the emotional stress of prolonged grief can cause physical and physiological changes in your body, which if left unresolved, predispose you to an increased risk of physical illness.

When you are in the acute stages of grief, the emotions you are experiencing engage your body's sympathetic nervous system (SNS) in the body's fight-or-flight response. When in fight mode, your body reacts as if you are preparing to confront an imminent threat to your safety.

The body is regulated by the autonomic system, which involves the SNS and the parasympathetic nervous system (PNS). The SNS activates the body's resources in fight mode, while the PNS helps the body to rest and recover. The SNS and the PNS are meant to balance each other, and the body is meant to spend the majority of its time in the PNS. Typically, all of this happens involuntarily in the body in response to stress. Most of the time we are not even aware of whether our SNS or our PNS is activated.

According to the Mayo Clinic, when the SNS is activated from a stressful event, your brain sets off an alarm system in your body. Through a combination of nerve and hormonal signals, the SNS prompts your adrenal glands to release adrenaline and cortisol, increasing your heart rate and elevating your blood pressure and respiratory rate. Cortisol, the primary stress hormone, curbs functions that would be nonessential or detrimental in a fight-or-flight situation. It alters immune system responses and suppresses the digestive system, the reproductive system, and growth processes. This complex natural alarm system also communicates with regions of your brain that control mood, motivation, and fear.

The SNS works well when responding to an acute crisis, but when it is continually activated in chronic stress situations, such as prolonged grief, the overexposure to cortisol and other stress hormones can disrupt almost all your body's processes. This chronic cascade of chemicals puts you at increased risk of numerous health problems, and also has the potential to shorten your life span. Some of the health problems resulting from chronic SNS stimulation are:

- Anxiety and depression
- Heart disease and stroke

- Immune system dysfunction
- Digestive problems
- Headaches and migraines
- Sleep problems
- Weight gain
- Memory and concentration impairment

The good news is that your PNS, which controls the "flight" side of your nervous system, can be activated to encourage relaxation and recovery of your body systems, taking you out of "fight" mode. According to Harvard Medical School, the PNS acts as a brake mechanism, dampening the stress response and converting the body's system back to homeostasis.

The PNS can be activated voluntarily, *if* you are aware that your SNS is being overly activated. By becoming aware that you have a say in whether your body is in a fight-or-flight state, you have the potential to preserve your future health. See Chapter 8 for methods to activate your PNS and decrease your stress level.

Clinical facts about the health impact of grief

According to data collected by Dr. Katherine Shear, director of Columbia University's Center for Complicated Grief, and Dr. Sidney Zisook, from the Department of Psychiatry, University of California, San Diego, "People with complicated grief have been found to be at increased risk for cancer, cardiac disease, hypertension, substance abuse, and suicidality" (Zisook 2009).

Dr. Holly Prigerson of Weill Cornell University stated, "It is not an exaggeration to say that many people experiencing prolonged grief (complicated grief) no longer see a point in living. The odds that a bereaved person will be suicidal are six times higher if he has PG. A desperate few take their own lives; many others seriously consider doing so. Some perish from medical illness in the wake of bereavement, literally or figuratively dying of a broken heart. PG is associated with heightened risks of heart attacks, cancer, and hospitalization for a serious health event, more disability days, dramatic increases in drinking and smoking and changes in eating." (Roth 2016)

If you believe you might have complicated grief, you should take it extremely seriously. Your health, and possibly your life, may depend on it.

PART 2

Conquering the Mountain of Grief

The Mountain of Grief

Grief can seem as unconquerable as Mt. Everest.
You have no climbing experience.
You aren't sure that you'll survive the elements
Or that you have the equipment you need
to safely climb the mountain.
Your very life is at stake.
You didn't set out to conquer mountains.
You didn't ask to be left out in the wild, un-
controllable elements of nature
But this is where you are.
Looking up at the formidable mountain of grief,
You feel overwhelmed and exhausted.
You feel defeated.
How do you even begin the climb?

Courage.
You may not feel courageous, but cour-
age is integral to your soul,
There, waiting for you to access it.
This courage is what will keep you moving,
Even when you feel like you'll never make it to the top.
You don't have to climb the mountain in one day, one year,
or even ten years.
But you do have to keep moving.
You feel alone on your climb, but you're not.
Guides who have climbed this mountain before await,
Those who can share how best to navigate its challenges.
Eventually, as you climb higher, your perspec-
tive on the mountain will start to change,
You'll see more clearly and realize

That what you thought was Mt. Everest
Is actually a smaller and more manageable mountain.
You realize you *can* do this.
You still have times where the mountain, once again,
seems unconquerable,
And you may need a day or two to re-
gain your courage. That's okay.
Climbing a mountain and overcoming grief
take courage, determination, and time.
The journey isn't about forgetting your loved one.
That will never happen.
The journey is to honor the love you shared
And find a way to carry your pain to
the top of the mountain,
Where your load will be bearable
And you can again experience joy in your life.
You can learn to live again.
Don't stay stuck halfway up the mountain.
Grief is hard work.
But you can make it to the top
One step at a time.

CHAPTER 6

When Grief Goes Wrong

Deep grief sometimes is almost like a specific location, a co-ordinate on a map of time. When you are standing in that forest of sorrow, you cannot imagine that you could ever find your way to a better place. But if someone can assure you that they themselves have stood in that same place, and now have moved on, sometimes this will bring hope.

—ELIZABETH GILBERT, EAT, PRAY, LOVE

GOOGLE THE DEFINITION for complicated grief and you will have a hard time finding one concrete answer or even a definition that a nonmedical person can easily understand. In my opinion, complicated grief doesn't have to be so complicated. To put it in simple terms, complicated grief occurs when grief has taken a wrong turn and is no longer healthy or functional grief. The griever is stuck in the acute stages of grief indefinitely. The signs of complicated grief can be seen as early as six months after the death of a loved one.

When you have lost someone you love, life as you know it stops in its tracks, and it will never be the same. This is a universal aspect of grief. Through time and the processing of emotions, the majority of grievers are able to accept the fact that their loved one is gone and able to take the steps necessary to heal enough to find meaningful life again. However, the griever who has complicated grief stays stuck in the acute stages of grief for years, sometimes decades, and this interferes with the ability to function in daily life. The person experiencing complicated grief is like a driver enroute to a faraway destination who has taken a wrong turn down a dead-end road and can't get turned back around to resume the journey. They are stuck, unable to process their emotions, and unable to adapt to life without their loved one.

This was me. And I can tell you that complicated grief is capable of sucking all the joy from your life. It is the hardest thing I have ever gone through in my life. Yet, I also want you to know that you don't have to live with the overwhelming and unrelenting pain I had. Effective therapies have been developed to help the complicated griever get back on the road to healthy grieving.

How do you know if you have Complicated Grief?

The pain of complicated grief became a type of prison for me; at times, it felt like a life sentence. I was stuck in my own hellish *Groundhog Day*, every day offering the same pain, a pain that overwhelmed all of my experiences. I could not find a way to move forward.

If you are experiencing complicated grief, there's a high probability that you have an intense yearning to have your loved one and your former life back. There may be times when you are downright angry that your loved one and the life you shared was taken from you. Reminders of your loved one may bring you so much pain that you find yourself avoiding places and activities you shared. Then, at other times, you are unable to stop looking at pictures or videos and thinking of your loved one.

If you are like me, you would give anything to be able to go back and be in your old life again. That is where you were happy—in the past with your loved one. And that is where you spend much of your time, in your memories, reliving that life.

Your yearning for your loved one is so strong that you can't see a future without them. So you hold out, hanging onto the life you once shared, certain that you can will it back into existence. But, regardless of how much you yearn for your loved one and your life with them, you can't go back. You are stuck, and unhappy, here in the present, alone without them.

You also might be confused. Maybe you aren't quite sure who you are without your loved one beside you and aren't able to envision how a life without them should look. Life seems to have lost its meaning.

This isn't how your life was supposed to be. Something has gone terribly wrong, and you want it fixed. Not only do you ruminate repeatedly about your life with your lost loved one, you also tend to isolate because you feel that no one can really understand the depth of your pain. All of these emotions combine to make it difficult for you to function and fulfill the normal daily activities that you were able to keep up with before the death of your loved one.

If any of this sounds familiar to you, and if it has been at least six months or a year since your loved one died, you might consider the possibility that you have complicated grief and that your grief has taken a wrong turn.

Clinical facts about Complicated Grief

An article by psychotherapist John Wilson, "The Nature of Complicated Grieving" (WIlson 2014), helped me to pinpoint the symptoms and risk factors for complicated grief.

Symptoms of Complicated Grief

According to the article, symptoms that are still occurring six months after the loss indicate that a griever is at increased risk for CG, such as:

- Persistent and invasive thoughts that disrupt daily activities
- Painful memories
- Inability to accept the finality of the death
- Intense yearning for the lost loved one
- Anger about the death
- Numbness or confusion,
- Loss of trust in others
- Isolation from others and loss of empathy
- Physical symptoms similar to those experienced by the deceased in their final illness
- Avoidance of reminders of the lost loved one
- Feeling that life is meaningless and hopeless without the loved one

Confirmed risk factors for Complicated Grief

- Death of a child or spouse
- Lack of family or social support
- History of anxiety or depression before the loss
- The death was violent or traumatic
- Issues around how they found out about the death
- History of marital dependency in loss of a spouse

Potential risk factors for Complicated Grief

- The griever is female
- The deceased died at a young age

- Death was sudden and unexpected
- Experience of multiple losses
- Loss is recent
- Family is not supportive

Dr. Katherine Shear, Director of the Center for Complicated Grief at the Columbia School of Social Work, has said that complicated grief is so intense that it actually changes the brain, and these changes can be seen on MRI. According to Dr. Shear,

> There are abnormalities in autobiographical memory, parts of the brain involving emotional regulation and other areas. And while those who grieve often suffer health problems in the early bereavement period, those who suffer from complicated grief have persistent health problems—from substance abuse and sleep disturbance to the potential for heart problems and even cancer (Williams 2015).

For those of us suffering with complicated grief, this information implies that the pain and stress of unresolved grief has made biological and physiological changes to both our brains and our bodies.

Dr. Shear encourages society to become educated about complicated grief. They need to understand that people who have CG are not "wallowing in grief," but are struggling with symptoms beyond their control.

According to studies done by Dr. Holly G. Prigerson from Weill Cornell Medical College in New York, seven to ten percent of grievers will end up struggling with complicated grief. Dr. Prigerson and her colleagues refer to complicated grief as prolonged grief disorder. Only time will tell whether complicated grief or prolonged grief disorder will prevail as the term to describe this grief phenomenon. I will continue referring to this experience as complicated grief until a definite term is decided amongst the professional community.

Dr. Prigerson describes complicated grief as:

> A grief that does not resolve naturally and persists far into the indefinite future as a defining feature severely adversely affecting the life of the survivor. The person is incapacitated by grief, so focused on the loss that it is difficult to care about much else. The bereaved ruminates about the death and longs for a reunion with the departed, feeling unsure who s/he is and where s/he fits in. Life is flat and cardboard, offering little meaning or purpose, and the future holds no prospect of joy, satisfaction or pleasure. S/he feels devalued and in constant turmoil, with an inability to accommodate to (if not a frank protest against) life without the beloved *(Prigerson and Raphael 2009)*

Dr. Prigerson was also involved in developing a scale for complicated grief, Inventory for Complicated Grief, which measures maladaptive symptoms of loss and is for use by clinical professionals for the diagnosis of complicated grief.

Dr. Prigerson and Weill Cornell Medical College have also developed a Grief Intensity Scale, which is a 12-question test that can be taken by grievers to indicate whether they may be developing complicated grief.

"Complicated grief is like a wound that doesn't heal and can follow the loss of any close relationship," Dr. Shear said in a *New York Times* article. Complicated grief, she said, rarely gets better on its own.

Dr. Shear states that antidepressants are frequently prescribed for people with intense grief reactions. Although they are sometimes helpful, she does not believe that drugs are the most effective way to treat this type of grief (Zisook, Grief and Bereavement: What psychiatrists need to know, 2009). Rather, a therapy she helped develop called Complicated Grief Treatment (CGT) achieves the most impressive results in a relatively short period of time.

Complicated Grief treatment

The treatment that Dr. Shear developed to treat complicated grief is a 16-session treatment that, clinical trials show, has significantly better outcomes than traditional supportive psychotherapy (D. K. Shear, n.d.).

Complicated Grief Treatment (CGT) is an evidence-based program, which means that it has been rigorously evaluated in three studies, funded by the National Institute of Mental Health, and has been shown to make positive and statistical differences in outcomes of people with complicated grief. According to study outcomes, CGT helps 70 percent of people, which makes it twice as effective as traditional talk therapy for those suffering from complicated grief (D. K. Shear, The Center for Complicated Grief).

Shorter than traditional therapy, CGT is completed over a four-month period. Dr. Shear describes the treatment, saying,

> We work with people to re-envision their own lives and to think about their long-term aspirational goals. We help them reconnect with other people in their lives and deepen the sense of connection with the deceased person and

increase their confidence in the durability of that connection. To achieve these goals the therapist asks people to revisit with the time of the death in imagination and reflect on that experience with the help of the therapist. We also ask that they start to revisit activities or situations they have been avoiding (Graham 2015).

According to Dr. Shear, the sixteen weekly sessions help those with complicated grief find ways to think about the death without the "intense feelings of anger, guilt or anxiety" they may have been experiencing before. They also function more effectively "by generating enthusiasm and creating plans for the future." CGT is highly structured. On a weekly basis, "patients are asked to monitor their grief reactions and are assigned specific homework activities to help them adapt to and accept the reality of their loss" (Graham 2015).

CGT helps people "reinvent their lives by revising goals and making plans" that do not include their lost loved ones, according to Dr. Shear (Graham 2015).

A colleague who collaborated with Dr. Shear on developing CGT, psychologist Allan Zuckoff, PhD, said in *Psychiatric News* that, "people with CG worry that if their grief goes away, they might forget the person who died or that it reflects that they didn't love the person as much as they believed." Zuckoff went on to explain, "An important aspect of the CGT process is affirming that we are not trying to extinguish the grief." He finished by saying, "We want people to be able to access memories of their loved one, but in a way that is more controlled and less dominated by pain" (Zisook, Grief and Bereavement: What psychiatrists need to know 2009).

Dr. Shear has said that she believes, "Grief is the form that love takes after someone you love dies." She continues, "The point isn't to put these feelings behind you altogether; that's not possible or even desirable. The point is to gain perspective and help grief find its rightful place in a person's life." Shear also said that, "Love never dies" (D. K. Shear, n.d.).

Finding a professional who understands that, ultimately, grief is about love and not just a clinical problem to be solved and "gotten over" is very important. As a medical professional myself, I believe that empathy plays a huge role in properly understanding and helping those who struggle with complicated grief find a way out of their pain.

Next steps to take if you believe you have CG

- Write down the symptoms you are having that are similar to those described above.
- Take your personal symptoms, along with the factual information about complicated grief, to your grief counselor and ask them to look into any certified therapists that administer CGT in the area where you live.
- If you are not already seeing a grief therapist, take the above information to your family practice/general physician and ask that they help you find a CGT therapist.
- If there is no one in your area who does CGT, go to the best qualified grief therapist or physician in your area, ask them to contact the Center for Complicated Grief, www.complicatedgrief.org, to look into specifics about CGT. The Center for Complicated Grief provides training for professionals.

When complicated grief really gets complicated

If you are as inquisitive as I was, you will probably look further into information on complicated grief. When you do, you will most likely be as concerned and shocked as I was to learn that the professional mental health and grief community is debating whether complicated grief should be included in the Diagnostic and Statistical Manual of Mental Disorders (DSM). Obviously, this means that complicated grief is being considered as a possible mental health disorder. This is where complicated grief really gets complicated.

Personally, I don't like the idea of my grief being labeled as a disorder or as a pathological mental health problem. I mean, come on. We have lost someone who meant the world to us. Some of us have lost multiple loved ones. Give us a break. We are grieving and our lives have been turned upside-down. But...while I don't appreciate my grief being labeled or having a time limit placed upon it, I can admit that I needed help and that the signs were there early on after my son died. I was in terrible pain, and I was not functioning in a healthy way. I also know from my research that most of us are not going to be able to get out of complicated grief on our own.

For the 10 percent of grievers who struggle with complicated grief, being officially diagnosed ensures that effective treatments will be available to them, and it increases the chances that insurance will cover these therapies. The significance of this component of the debate is huge. By allowing complicated grief to be added into the DSM, these grievers will receive the targeted therapies that can help them get back onto the path of healthy grief. As a survivor of complicated grief, it is my personal opinion that the benefits of including complicated grief into the DSM far outweigh the disadvantages.

However, I also want to say that I don't believe we should neatly place complicated grief into a medical journal, develop a treatment, and call it good. I want to take a look at what I believe is a large contributing factor to the development of complicated grief. I believe that our Western society has inadvertently and negatively influenced the grief experience.

Is it possible that one source of the problem of grievers falling into prolonged and complex grief could be related to the fact that we live in a society that denies and is uncomfortable with death and grief? And that this denial of the griever's pain makes the process of grieving so much harder?

Myths of grief

- Everything happens for a reason.
- God doesn't give you more than you can handle.
- Time will heal your wounds and you will "get over" your loss.
- You will return to "normal" after you have healed.
- You can replace your lost loved one.
- Faith will get you through.
- Suffering makes you stronger.
- Other people can take away your pain for you.
- All losses are the same.
- You can outrun your pain.
- You will always be able to count on loved ones for support.
- If you have emotional outbursts or intense emotions you must be losing your mind.
- You are weak if you show your emotions in public.
- The pain of your loss will come to an end.
- You can expect to go through specific stages.

- You shouldn't act sad around others because it makes them feel bad.
- You shouldn't talk about your lost loved one because others don't know what to say.

Don't listen to the myths of grief. Listen to the truth within your heart.

CHAPTER 7

The Emotional Reality of Grief

That's the thing about pain, it demands to be felt.

—JOHN GREEN

SOCIETY'S IMAGE OF grief is pretty simple: You, the griever, are sad and to recover, you must find a way to "get over" your sadness within an appropriate amount of time.

If only grief were this simple.

You should be prepared for the reality that grief will drag you through a myriad of emotions—from the raw, debilitating, and shocking wound of your immediate loss to the long-term feelings of loneliness, isolation, and longing for your loved one that never quite go away. You may also be caught off guard when your emotions change rapidly, intensifying and then retreating again, only to reemerge when you least expect them. This is the reality of grief.

The emotions you undergo during grief will possibly be the most painful and confusing experiences you will ever have. Grief can leave a path of destruction so wide and overwhelming that it feels as if you will never recover. However, understanding the grief process and the emotional fallout that can occur can better equip you to deal with your pain.

Most grievers are vulnerable when exposed to all of these complex emotions. Not only are you confused by what you are going through, but others around you don't understand, either. All these feelings may combine to make you feel as if you are going crazy.

News flash—you are not crazy. You are grieving. And if you are like me, at times it feels as if you are fighting for your very survival.

Surviving the storm

You cannot control the emotions of grief any more than you can control the weather. You can, however, prepare for the storm that you know is coming. Awareness and preparation can help you survive the storm: awareness of the scope of emotions you will experience and preparation for the inevitable fallout that these emotions can cause. You can stock up on supplies to take care of yourself during the storm and persevere through the onslaught of pain when you know that sometimes the acute, destructive stage of a storm lasts longer than you anticipated.

Eventually, you will look at your life in two stages: before the storm and after the storm.

Loss will change you. I mean this literally. After you have lost someone you love, you will never be the same again. I look back with an almost nostalgic sadness at photos of me before my losses. I know that the images are me, but I feel as if I'm looking at a stranger. Before the losses, I was carefree and glowingly happy, always positive and confident, certain that there was nothing I couldn't handle in life. I was a different person, then. That woman no longer exists. I vaguely recall what it felt like to be her, naïve and secure in the future, and I'm glad I got to experience the innocence and trust that everything was going to work out as planned, at least for a little while. But honestly, a part of me wishes I could somehow go back in time to warn the happy and lighthearted woman in the pictures that a heartache so big, so unfathomable, was headed her way. Looking at the pictures now, I can't help but feel sorry for her, knowing all of the struggles awaiting her.

The emotions of my storm

My late-husband's death was the beginning of my emotional downfall. After he died, I was unprepared for the misery I found myself in. Despondency seemed to engulf my life within a dark shroud. Everything was a struggle. I had never felt so hopeless.

Lost, heartbroken, powerless, and in denial: these are the words that really stand out for me as I describe this time. I was sure there must be some mistake. How could my young, loving, and vibrant husband die? We had so much living left to do.

After a year of severe heartbreak, I slowly began to repair my life and my family. I still remained sad and in pain, but I was able to find some joy again. I had survived, but every part of my life had been damaged.

When my son died two years later, initially I thought I understood what his loss would feel like because of what I had gone through after losing Steve. I have never been so wrong. This time my grief was like an EF-5 tornado (I'm a Kansas girl who grew up in tornado alley), destroying everything in its path, especially me. My emotions were out of control. The familiar emotions I had experienced after Steve's death—sadness, despair, and loneliness—re-emerged, but along with them came a new onslaught of negative emotions I felt I must attempt to restrain.

I was experiencing moments of a mother's panic. Where was my son? Was he safe? Was he afraid? My maternal drive to protect him was still so strong that at times I felt as if I might lose my mind with worry. Panic and terror are the emotions I felt when I realized I could no longer protect my son.

Envy isn't the right word to describe the emotion I felt when I spent time with friends and relatives whose families were whole, but that is the closest emotion I can find. Being with families who were still able to enjoy their loved ones reminded me of the vacant spots in my family and made it difficult to participate in such occasions. I began to isolate to avoid these painful reminders.

One situation I recall happened about a year after Jordan died. I had family friends who were struggling because their youngest son had gone off to college, and they were empty nesters. They said they were "grieving" and that they were having a hard time coping. I was deeply upset that they were able to use the same word to describe their son's change of address as the one I used to describe the pain associated with my son's death. This new and surprisingly cynical and bitter side of me screamed internally, "Are you kidding me? You should try burying your son and then see how you feel." I know, it's not pretty. I'm thankful I never shared my thoughts with them. Now, I can look back and agree that they were indeed experiencing a type of grief; their life had changed because their son was moving into his adult life. Even though that type of grief can't be compared to the death of a child, I can recognize now that they had the right to grieve that change in their lives. I didn't own a patent on grief.

Other new emotions that emerged were anger, irritability, and resentment. How could this have happened? What had I done to deserve losing both my husband and son? I felt I was being punished, even though I had lived by all the rules. My anger at times was scorching and white-hot; I could almost feel the heat of it radiating out from my body. It took everything I had to keep the anger contained. I wasn't always successful, and unfortunately, many times it was directed at those closest to me.

My anger turned into skepticism and resentment. I felt resentment against life and God; resentment against everything and almost everyone. I experienced heart-wrenching guilt and regrets about all of the emotional and physical pain my son had gone through. The regrets almost took me down. I became skeptical of life and was bitter for several years. I no longer recognized my life anymore or the person I saw in the mirror. Death, grief, and loss had changed everything.

What you can expect from the storm

There is so much more to grief than just sadness. You should be prepared for the vast array of feelings you may have to deal with during your grieving.

- Shock
- Guilt
- Anger
- Irritability
- Rage
- Despair
- Regret
- Anxiety
- Loneliness
- Denial
- Skepticism
- Resentment
- Yearning
- Sadness
- Worry
- Isolation

- Self-pity
- Envy
- Fear
- Hopelessness

These are just a few of the negative feelings you may experience. The actual scope of what is possible is almost endless. If these are not acknowledged and eventually worked through, they will pull you down into the quicksand of grief, each one like a weight attached to your ankle. Every griever will experience different emotions at different intensities and of varying lengths. The grieving process is subjective and quite personal. There is no wrong or right way to grieve.

Regardless of what society expects of us grievers, our hearts and emotions refuse to follow the binding and impossible constraints and timelines placed upon us. Grief demands that our emotions and heartache be adequately attended to, honored, and healed before we are allowed to move forward. And after we are able to heal, still we will always carry our loss with us. Life will be different. You will be different. This is the truth of grief.

Don't allow society to put your grief into a narrow box. Be gentle with your broken heart. Pain and loss will change you, but they don't have to define you.

Grief as a raw nerve

I want to tell you a story that had a tremendous effect on me. It is the story of Madonna Badger, a successful business woman and mother of three who seemed to have everything in life going for her. On Christmas morning of 2011, a fire broke out in the early hours in the home she was renovating. The fire killed her three young daughters and both of her parents. Her entire family was gone in a matter of minutes. In her article in *Vogue Magazine,* "The Long Road Back: How to Keep Going When the Unimaginable Happens," she describes her descent into hell:

> I broke down and experienced what mental-health experts call a 'suicide gesture'—I grabbed a bottle of pills and threatened to take them. I hadn't been in my body since the fire, and now I seemed to be floating somewhere else, with no emotional muscle, no ability to fend off anything, and I was soon committed to an acute-care unit, a psychiatric hospital in New Canaan, Connecticut. I couldn't check myself out.
>
> I spent some time at what was billed as a trauma-therapy center outside Nashville, by which time my hair was coming out in clumps. I don't remember eating. At times I was manic; at other times, almost catatonically depressed. At one point, I cried out to a therapist, "I need somebody to help take care of me. I need to talk to somebody. I need help" (Badger 2013).

She was eventually connected to the director of the Psychiatric Research Institute at the University of Arkansas, Dr. Richard Smith. Dr. Smith assured Madonna that she wasn't crazy; she was grieving. He said that within six weeks, he and his staff would help her find the tools to help her get through the beginning of the pain.

Dr. Smith told her that when a child dies, it's as if a giant nerve has been severed—in her case, three giant nerves, as well as the nerves that connected her to her parents. He said that though these are raw nerves, little by little they'd grow new skin over them so they wouldn't be as agonizingly painful as they were at that moment.

This image of grief as a raw nerve made a lot of sense to me. I finally understood why I felt I was walking around with my heart open and exposed. Any insensitive comment or action by another caused an irritation and imparted a pain that was almost unbearable. When you are walking around with a raw nerve, you get to a point where you just have to limit its exposure to insensitive and painful experiences and protect yourself during the healing process.

Eventually, with nurturing and time, the nerve can re-grow a new sheath to cover the exposed endings. Although it will never be as strong and protected as it was before the loss, it can provide some protection against the moments of grief and pain that will inevitably continue to happen.

Madonna Badger has shown us that even after the most horrific and tragic losses, we can find a way to get through the pain and survive. Our hearts will never be the same, but we can find our way to some semblance of life again by respecting our pain and emotions, our memories, our lost loved ones, and ourselves.

CHAPTER 8

Practical Tools for self-Care in Your Grief

Keep love in your heart. A life without it is like a sunless garden when the flowers are dead.

—OSCAR WILDE

WHILE WE EACH grieve differently, I do have a few practical suggestions that helped me through my grief. Take any of the suggestions that feel right and leave the rest. Search your heart for what will help you heal.

Above all, be kind and patient with yourself.

Caring for yourself, emotionally and physically, will help as you learn to manage your grief. Do your best to maintain your physical health, for that will give you the strength you need to tackle your grief every day. If you allow your health to deteriorate, you are just adding another challenge to overcome. Ultimately, this will prolong your grieving process.

Few things in life are as physically and emotionally exhausting as grief. You will not be able to do all of the things you did before.

Be patient with yourself. Listen to the signals your body is sending you. Care for yourself during this time as you would care for your dearest loved one.

Give yourself permission to grieve.

The death of someone you love is not something you will get over in a few weeks or even a few months. Most of us never get over the pain of our loss, ever; it is just something we learn to live with. Be realistic about your grief. Grief is a brutal journey that requires a lot of work, courage, and determination. There is no hurry. Do not base your grieving on what others expect of you. We all grieve differently.

Ask for help.

When you are dealing with grief, you will find that everyday activities you once accomplished with ease now feel like expeditions to conquer Mt. Everest. Find those few people you know you can count on and let them know you are struggling. Maybe you can ask for help getting your kids to after-school activities or help doing paperwork and paying your bills. We all need help sometimes. Most people who are trying to support you don't know how to do that. Hands are reaching out to help you. Give them a specific task that might help you feel less overwhelmed.

Surround yourself with people who understand loss.

Being part of a support group and knowing that others are going through the same type of pain as you can help relieve the loneliness of the grief journey. Modern-day access to the internet has made it easier than ever to find support. Something as simple as Googling *grief* can bring a treasure trove of resources directly to you, no matter where you are. There are interactive support groups on Facebook and other social media sites. Use these resources.

I tried going to grief support groups in my area but never found the right fit for me. It is possible that more resources are available in your area. Check out your local resources and find out if they work for you.

Engage in comforting activities.

What is it that brings you some modicum of happiness? I discovered that watching HGTV and then repainting some of the rooms in my house was very therapeutic. While painting, I listened to self-help and spiritual audiobooks. The repetitive motions involved in painting, along with the inspiration to make some changes in my life, significantly encouraged and comforted me.

I also found great joy in being with my two-year-old niece. Her innocent joy in life was infectious and made me feel very happy. While spending time with her, I was able to reconnect with the child who was still inside me and wanted to be happy. My niece brought me hope that I could feel joy again.

Think about what might be helpful for you. Maybe it's working in the garden, or volunteering, or exercising. Find what brings you some joy and make yourself do it.

Be mindful of the energy you allow around you.

Grief puts you in a fragile state, and you absorb any negativity that may be around you. Surround yourself with people who can be empathetic with the pain you're experiencing. If someone says something insensitive once, assume that it was unintentional and make yourself let it go. However, if someone is consistently insensitive or hurtful, do not be around them. You must make your well-being a priority. Hurtful words and negative energy turn into a toxic mess that will only pull you down further. Protect yourself. When you are with others, imagine an energy field surrounding and protecting your body. Identify the people in your life who are positive supports, and create time in your schedule to spend with them.

Put boundaries on insensitive and toxic behavior.

There is a pain that is secondary to grief that can rub salt into your wounds and make it even more difficult to heal. I am talking about the pain that occurs when others, relatives or friends, minimize or do not see, understand, or acknowledge the pain and struggle you are going through. I wasn't prepared for the deep anguish that this insensitivity brought me. In such situations, you are left to make the decision as to whether the ongoing pain that a person is causing is worth continuing to allow them into your life. Here are a couple of things to consider:

First, if someone has said something hurtful or behaved in a way that causes you pain, monitor the relationship, and protect your energy. If the insensitive and hurtful behavior occurs more than a few times, that person is showing you a pattern that can become toxic and impede your healing.

Second, you will have to decide what action you should take based on the significance of your relationship. Family members should not be walked away from easily, but you can limit your time with them and prepare yourself emotionally and energetically when you have to be around them.

Of course, you should be able to discuss the situation with the rational people in your life. Let them know how hurtful their statements or actions have been to you. In my personal experience, most people who behave in this manner are just that, insensitive and hurtful; very few are willing to acknowledge that they did anything that could have hurt you. These are the people that will leave you feeling as if you've been hit by a truck. I had to excise a few people from my life, like a surgeon removing a cancerous tumor from my body. They were emotionally draining the life out of me. My survival was more important than not hurting anyone's feelings.

Treasure the people in your life who can empathize with you and understand your ongoing struggles. These supporters are rare, but they are out there. They should be recognized for the blessings they are.

Get out of your comfort zone.

When I was in grief, I wanted nothing more than to stay isolated and sheltered in my house, not having to interact with anyone. This is fine when your grief is new and you are trying to get over the initial shock and trauma of your loss. But be wary of falling into a pattern of isolating from life. Make a commitment to get out of your normal routine so that you have to engage with others. You may do that by going to the gym, volunteering, or joining a support group, a gardening group, or an exercise group. Do something that takes you out of the comfort zone of your routine and out of the emotional patterns that your grief has locked you into.

Others may be uncomfortable around your grief.

It is so hard not to take this personally, but the truth is that our society has not prepared most of us to be comfortable around others who are struggling with grief or illness. Don't be caught off guard when people you thought you could count on for support let you down. It really isn't about you; it's about them. Taking on the additional pain that this can cause will only intensify your overall pain and grief. To be able to grieve authentically, you must surround yourself with people who can simply be with you while you are in your pain.

Get comfortable with saying no.

Most likely, you will not be able to keep up with all of the activities you were able to do before your loss. Don't beat yourself up because of it. Learn that it really is okay if you are not able to do it all. Once again, listen to your body and your emotions on this one. When you are asked to do something, what is your immediate response? If the request creates a sense of anxiety, realize that you have the right to say, "I'm not able to do that, right now."

Practice saying this out loud if you need to. Guilt is a big part of our discomfort when it comes to saying no. We place too many expectations on ourselves, and we believe we should still be able to do it all, no matter what. Let the guilt go. Learn to say no.

Don't bottle up your emotions.

Tears do not mean that you're weak. Tears are healing. According to Dr. Judith Orloff:

> Tears are a sign of strength, courage and authenticity, they help to heal the heart and to emotionally clear sadness and stress. Crying is also essential to resolve grief. Tears help us process the loss so we can keep living with open hearts. Otherwise, we are a set up for depression if we suppress these potent feelings (Orloff 2011).

Biochemist Dr. William Frey at the Ramsey Medical Center in Minneapolis discovered that tears that are generated from emotions like grief facilitate the removal of stress hormones from our body. After studying the composition of tears, Dr. Frey found that emotional tears shed these hormones and other toxins that accumulate during stress. Additional studies show that crying releases "positive" hormones called endorphins into our bloodstream, allowing for temporary, natural relief of pain (Collier 2014).

Researchers concluded that tears can lower our stress levels. Trying to suppress your tears because you think they are a sign of weakness will only increase your stress levels and potentially can contribute to stress-causing illnesses. Don't be ashamed to cry. Crying is your body's natural response for healing your pain (Collier 2014).

Grief has ups and downs

Don't let down days catch you unaware. No matter how much time has passed since the death of your loved one, you will still have days that are hard. Remember the old cliché "one step forward and two steps back," because it really does apply to grief. Do your best to stay in tune with your body and your emotions. Don't place unnecessary pressure or guilt on yourself on the days you are upset or unable to complete the tasks you have set.

Activate your relaxation response regularly.

While you are doing the work to heal your broken heart, make sure you are engaging your parasympathetic nervous system regularly to counteract the stress that your grief is putting your body through. Not only will this possibly help your healing, but it will ensure that when you are ready to live life again, your body will be able to support you.

Here are a few ways to engage the parasympathetic nervous system:

- Deep breathing, biofeedback mechanisms
- Meditation
- Yoga
- Spending time in nature
- Spending time with children or others who make you happy
- Visualization techniques for relaxation
- Mild exercise
- Massage

Becoming aware of the connection between our emotional and physical states can pave the way to healing. Grief is a process. We must work through it; we cannot escape it. We must recognize and honor our emotions and our pain in order to be healed. But if your grief is prolonged and you are struggling, please be aware of the impact this stress is having on your physical health and take steps to reduce the possibility of long-term health problems. Your future self will thank you.

Prepare for downtime on holidays and special occasions.

Special days that you used to celebrate with your lost loved ones are likely to become days you dread and have to get through, rather than occasions you can continue to celebrate and enjoy. The reality is that few times during the year is our loved one's absence more deeply felt and mourned than during holidays, birthdays, and anniversaries.

The reminder of your loss is never so obvious as when these dates roll around and you are either alone or surrounded by extended family and friends whose families are whole and together. Your family, on the other hand, has an obvious vacant spot and will never be whole again without your missing loved one. Just as the death of a loved one changes the way we look at life, these special days will never be the same again without them there by our side.

Here are a few things I want to share with you:

GETTING THROUGH THE DAY IS ENOUGH.

Know this: you do not have to do the grief work of healing on these special days. You just have to get through them. You can pick back up on the work to heal your grief after the day is over. Understand that it really is okay to feel sad. You are in pain, and you can't move through the pain until you've respected the emotions that demand to be felt.

LISTEN TO WHAT YOUR BODY AND EMOTIONS ARE TELLING YOU.
I tried to ignore my feelings of loss and sadness and focus on the festivities, but my physical body did not cooperate. Instead, it reminded me that, ultimately, I'm not the one in control. It shut itself down, making me physically ill, and it took days for me to recover my physical strength. Emotions are the precursor to physical symptoms.

IT IS OKAY TO SAY NO.
It is okay to say no to a family gathering or to leave early if you are not tolerating it well. Be careful about isolating yourself, though. That is not helpful, either. Find the balance that helps you get through the day.

REMEMBER THE DAYS YOU SHARED.
Remember the beautiful days you were blessed to share with your loved ones before they died. What amazing gifts they were.

Place a limit on the time you spend grieving.

This is a really hard one, I know. If it has been more than a year since the loss of your loved one, do your best to control the amount of daily time that you spend actively mired in the pain of grief. I look back now and see that I lost years of my life because I didn't believe that I had any control over my thoughts and feelings. Basically, my thoughts and feelings controlled me. Allow yourself a time during the day to feel the pain. During this time, try to make yourself remember not only the loss, but also the love and wonderful experiences you shared with your loved one.

In the novel *The Girl from the Train* (Joubert 2015), I read an idea that had great appeal to me. The book described the use of a mourning blanket after a loved one's death. You set aside several hours during the day and wrap yourself up in the blanket, imagining that your lost loved one is in there with you and that you are grieving the loss together. After the blanket is put away, the griever gets on with the business of daily living. Using an item like a blanket is a physical reminder that you have control over the amount of time you allow yourself to actively grieve throughout the day. It doesn't mean that you forget or pretend that your pain isn't real. It means that you also recognize that you must learn how to live and function with the pain.

In complicated grief, our default memories about our lost loved one are usually the painful ones surrounding the loss. Change that default picture! Remember the love. And then remember that love cannot be lost. There are times when the grief will hit you out of nowhere. You're fine one moment and on your knees the next. Reread the guidelines above. Give yourself time to feel the pain that is demanding to be felt, but then add the positive memories into the equation. Eventually, you will get to a point where you can smile while you shed tears.

REMEMBER TO FOCUS ON THE LOVE.

You can start by recognizing how very fortunate you were to ever have experienced this strong bond of love. Some people never have such a meaningful and life-changing love. Remembering the love you no longer have is painful and very difficult in the beginning of your grief. Eventually, though, you can make a conscious effort to choose to remember your loved one with gratitude for the experiences you were given. This love was a gift that you were blessed to have received. You must not take the gift for granted by only remembering the pain of your loss, for when love and loss walk together, the pain is more tolerable.

CREATE A REMINDER OF YOUR LOVE.

One way you can do this is by creating some type of personal memorial of the shared joy and love you experienced with your loved one. This memorial will look different for each of us. It can be a video, a journal, an online blog, a photo montage—the options are endless. I created a scrap book of my life with my late husband and son and documented my treasured memories. I can go back through them now, almost a decade later, and remember with great love the moments we were so blessed to share together. There is no physical item that is more precious to me than this scrapbook. Honestly, the scrapbook is more than just a physical possession; it is a living symbol of the love and experiences I shared with my husband and son, experiences that, when I remember and honor them, can help relieve my pain.

We also had teddy bears made for Maggie out of Steve's shirts. She treasures these bears and sometimes uses them to fall asleep at night.

WRITE DOWN YOUR FEELINGS.

You will be surprised at how therapeutic it can be to journal your experience. The pen can be an outlet for expressing your pain, letting it flow out of you and onto the paper.

If you have unresolved feelings concerning your loved one or something left unsaid, consider writing them a letter about what you wish you could have discussed with them. You can even write a dialogue, including what you believe their response would have been. Sometimes this can help you let go of unresolved issues.

You can also use journaling to create a collection of memories you shared with your lost loved one.

SPEND TIME IN NATURE.

Fresh air and sunshine have a healing effect on our bodies. Sunshine is full of healing energy. Sometimes when the weather isn't cooperating or I don't have enough energy to go outside, I remember one of my favorite outdoor experiences. I was walking in nature on a beautiful spring day. The sun was strong enough that when I was in its direct light, I was hot. A gentle breeze helped. I came to a heavily treed area where lush, thick, green grass grew beneath the trees. I lay down for a break. The grass was as cushy and soft as a down mattress. The breeze playing in the shade was the perfect temperature. As I lay there under the trees, surrounded by a bright-blue sky, the newly sprouted leaves blowing in the wind, I felt a remarkable sense of peace and comfort, as if Mother Nature herself was embracing me. I always go back to this memory when I need some emotional relief and relaxation.

ADEQUATE SLEEP IS VITAL.

The emotional anguish of grief can cause sleep disturbances. A lack of sleep makes it more difficult to deal with grief. Insomnia is a vicious cycle that can make it harder to work through your grief. If you are struggling just to get six or seven hours of sleep, take steps to improve your sleep. Here are some ideas for you to try.

- Try not to fall asleep thinking about painful memories of your loss.
- Make a conscious effort to think of an experience that brings you happiness or comfort. It can be a happy memory of your loved one or a memory of an experience that brought you peace, like my memory of resting under the trees.
- Do a guided visualization. Imagine you are on a beach or in a flower garden surrounded by shade trees. We all have

our own idea of what a peaceful experience looks like. Find your peaceful experience.

- Talk with your physician before taking any supplements, as they could interact with prescription medications you might be taking. Your physician can also give you suggestions to help with insomnia.

EXERCISE HELPS, TOO.

Exercise releases endorphins, the feel-good chemicals, into your body, and can help blunt the stress response we feel during grief. Mild exercise also can help encourage a healthy sleep pattern. Do your best to engage in some physical activity, even if it's just a ten-minute walk on the treadmill or outside.

> **Reminder: Be kind and patient with yourself during your grief process.**

Cautions while grieving

Sometimes, we grievers unknowingly involve ourselves in activities as a way of distracting from our pain. Sometimes it takes a while to realize that there is no way to avoid the pain; it just waits patiently while we busily focus on something else.

Be aware that some activities may bring you a false sense of happiness and can potentially develop into destructive habits. Doing things like shopping in excess, drinking alcohol in excess, eating in excess, working in excess, or jumping right into another relationship may bring you an initial sense of relief because it temporarily distracts you from your pain, but the pain will still be waiting for you to deal with after the rush of adrenaline experienced from these activities dies down and reality rushes back in. At that point, it is possible that you will have even more issues to deal with than grief, making your healing process all the more difficult.

CHAPTER 9

How Western Society's Denial of Death Complicates Grief

It is difficult to accept death in this society because it is unfamiliar. In spite of the fact that it happens all the time, we never see it.

—*ELISABETH KUBLER-ROSS (E. KUBLER-ROSS 1975)*

DEATH AND GRIEF are universal. They touch all genders. All races. All religions. They don't discriminate based on socioeconomic status or age. Death and grief do not care if you are a mother, father, spouse, child, sibling, or friend. Eventually, we will all be touched by death. There is no life without death. They are two sides of the same coin.

Your experience of the death of a loved one will be different based on the area of the world you live in, as well as the religion, spirituality, belief in the afterlife or lack thereof that you practice. In our Western culture, death is a part of life that we sweep under the proverbial rug. The subconscious denial and fear of death in our society is not an effective coping mechanism. It leads to unnecessary suffering.

If you are a widow or a parent who has lost a child, you know that most people are uncomfortable around you. They don't know what to say to you. This only adds another layer onto your already complex pain. I don't believe people intentionally ostracize. The truth is, you are a glaring reminder to others that the same untimely and tragic loss could happen to them as well, so they keep you at arm's length so they can avoid the distressing reminder that comes along with seeing you.

Surface dwellers in the West

Our Western society is not only a death-denying culture, but a pain-denying culture. We are uncomfortable with anything messy. Just for starters, we try to avoid seeing aging, illness, poverty, death, and grief. We have developed a subconscious aversion to anything that makes us feel negative emotions. We have become a society that values and protects our comfortable, structured, and insulated lives. We believe in "positive thinking" as the way to avoid pain in life.

People like their lives wrapped up nice and neat and don't want the chaos and unseemliness of watching others deal with pain and suffering. Many people will go to great lengths to avoid being reminded of death and pain, as if they were contagious diseases; as if by staying away from them, they can avoid contracting pain and death themselves. They are fine supporting their loved one for the first few weeks, maybe even months, but when the pain lingers, it is not accepted as easily.

Unfortunately for us grievers who are experiencing these life-altering challenges, the subconscious alienation by those from whom we had hoped for support only further increases our suffering. The griever's life is in pieces, yet we are often left on our own to try to put the pieces together again.

I have come up with a name for people who, in order to keep their own lives clean, tidy, and predictable, avoid the suffering of others. I call them surface dwellers. Surface dwellers don't want to look too deeply into any undesired situation in life lest it cause discomfort and anxiety. Surface dwellers like to skim across the surface of life, where everything seems safe and reliable and no emotion gets too messy.

I'm sure I sound bitter, or at the very least, harsh, but I can also say that I don't believe the insensitivity of surface dwellers is intentional or even considered on a conscious level. Our Western culture has gradually shifted from a death-aware society to a death-denying society, inadvertently creating a plethora of surface dwellers.

At one time, we grievers also lived up on the surface, and we were naïve, as well, believing that our happiness and family were guaranteed. Surface dwellers live within an illusion, just as we once did, believing that they have control over the circumstances of their lives. Who are we to crush their fantasies with reality? Can we really blame them for wanting to stay on the surface for as long as they can?

Pain and loss quickly drag you down from the surface of life. They suck you deep underneath, down to the very core, where the anguish and struggle are ruthless and unavoidable. We are relentlessly churned through the raw emotions and heart-crushing reality of loss. Eventually, when we have been thoroughly processed to the core, our load is lightened a bit, finally allowing us to rise upwards. We will never be wide-eyed and naïve enough to live on the surface again. We have experienced the inescapable truth of our human existence and understand that pain and loss are inevitable. The weight of this knowledge keeps us anchored, whether we want to be or not.

Bearing witness to grief

If, as a culture, we don't bear witness to grief, the burden of loss is placed entirely on the bereaved, while the rest of us avert our eyes and wait for those in mourning to stop being sad, to let go, to move on, to cheer up. And if they don't – if they have loved too deeply, if they do wake each morning thinking, **I cannot continue to live** – well, then we pathologize their pain; we call their suffering a disease. We do not help them. We tell them that they need to get help (Cheryl Strayed 2015)**.**

Grief is a complex process that affects each of us differently. We have loved ones who play roles in our lives—some more significant than others. Your marriage is not like your neighbor's marriage. Your relationship with your parents is not like your friends' relationships with their parents. How do we define what it really feels like to be a widow or to lose a child when it is such a subjective experience, an experience based on that particular relationship? Sure, there are universal aspects of grief we all endure, but just as no two snowflakes are alike, I believe that every grief path is individual. Grief that may be a slight disturbance in one person's life can be a game-stopper in another's.

Grief is a messy and chaotic process that doesn't proceed in an orderly fashion. Sometimes I think our Western society has laid out categories for the milestones we should expect in life. I imagine the categories as looking something like this:

- Childhood
- God and religion
- Education
- Friendships
- Career
- Love
- Marriage
- Parenthood
- Retirement
- Eventual death in old age

Western society teaches us to believe that if we live according to the rules, life will remain predictable and under our control. Unexpected death, illness, and grief are not acknowledged in our structured and categorized lives; they are just something we are supposed to fit in. When death does suddenly happen to someone we love, society subliminally sends us the message that we are expected to quietly bear our pain while still maintaining our daily lives and to "get over" our grief in a timely manner while not unnecessarily disrupting anyone else's life.

Despite these expectations, our hearts and emotions refuse to follow the constraints and timeline that society has set. We grievers don't want to have to pretend we are okay when we are not okay. We don't want to act as if we don't miss our lost loved one, because we do. We don't want to have to walk on eggshells when someone doesn't know what to say to us; we are already walking a tightrope and barely keeping our balance. We already feel alone and don't want to be further isolated by those around us just because our lives have fallen outside of life's expected categories.

Society's expectations of grievers are unrealistic. For a griever who has lost a loved one who was a vital part of their life, nothing will ever be the same. Life is turned upside-down. It doesn't matter what society expects of us, because grief demands that our emotions and heartache be adequately attended to and healed before we are allowed to move forward in life. Even after we are able to move onward, we will always live with the void and pain of the death of our loved one. We just learn to make room in our lives for the pain.

The time between birth and death

Most of us live as if we have all the time in the world. Death is something that happens to other people, not to us. Despite our cultural denial of death, not one of us will escape our human existence without dying. And few will escape without the loss of someone they love.

As much as we want to believe that we have control over our lives, it's a fantasy. Really, we can rely on only two certainties—birth and death. What really matters in this lifetime is what we chose to do with the time between those two events. If we pay attention, death has much to teach us about life.

In Western society, birth and death are the two most documented events in life. We can go to any cemetery, any historical library, or even through a search on the internet, to find information on the dates of birth and death on almost any person who has lived in the past several centuries. My question is, what happened between these two dates? Why do we measure the number of years that we lived as the ultimate success? Can we not look at the inevitability of death and ultimately let it guide the decisions we make about how we live? Do we miss out on fully living life because we fear death?

In *The Denial of Death* (Becker 1973), Ernest Becker posits that our fear of death is actually an underlying fear of life. To contemplate our own physical death requires that we engage in a little self-reflection on how we are living our lives. Exactly what are we doing with the time we are given for this human experience here on earth? Most people don't like being reminded that our time is limited or that we might not be making the most of it.

Our days in a physical body are numbered. To honor life, we have to stop living as if our time is endless. We have a choice to make. We can go forward mindlessly, letting each day pass by unrecognized, or we can live our days aware of the gift of life that is within us in each moment. We shouldn't take even the bad days for granted. If death can teach us anything, it is that while we are alive, we can embrace life by living our days mindfully, maintaining awareness that nothing is promised to us or to our loved ones. This very moment is the only certain thing.

Collectively, the moments we experience create a lifetime. Are you happy with how you've spent your lifetime so far? Are you doing your best to value each moment? Somewhere along the way, we seem to become so preoccupied with the superficial tasks of living that we miss the bigger meaning of life.

Undeniable statistics: We all die

During the average lifetime, based on the average resting respiratory rate of 16 breaths per minute, we inhale and exhale 662 million times. How many of these breaths are we truly present for?

How many of them have we taken for granted, believing we have an infinite number of breaths left?

The average American lifespan is 78.7 years (Post 2013), which amounts to a whopping 28,744 days. I suppose that sounds like a lot until you subtract the number of days you've already lived. At 48 years old, I have already lived 17,531 days, leaving me a grand total of...drum roll, please...10,957 days. That is, *if* I live to the average age.

Here are a few more numbers on death for your contemplation. They come from the Ecology Global Network (Network n.d.):

- 2 people die every second
- 6,316 people die every hour
- 151,600 people die every day
- 55.3 million people die every year

I'm not trying to cause any more anxiety about death. The point I want to make is that, whether we admit it or not, death is occurring all around us. So, what drives our denial of this obvious fact?

According to psychologist James Gire:

> Death anxiety is a multifaceted construct that is not easy to define but has been conceptualized to include: fear of death of oneself, fear of death of others, fear of dying of self, and fear of the dying of others. Fear of death has to do with the fear of the event of death and comprises such things as what happens to the individual after the experience of death. To some, it could be fear about judgment – whether one would go to heaven or hell, or what might happen to people and possessions that one may leave behind,

including one's spouse, children, and businesses. The fear of dying refers to the process of dying and anxiety about how they will die. Anxieties here revolve around the notions of wasting away, and the pain that may be associated with dying. (Gire n.d.)

Gire also proposes that death anxiety can happen on several different levels: public, private, and non-conscious. Most of us are not even aware of our death anxiety. One of the most obvious ways in which we display death anxiety is through our avoidance.

Theories on western society's denial of death

Dr. Elisabeth Kubler Ross

One of the foremost pioneers of the twentieth century on the study of death and dying was Dr. Elisabeth Kubler-Ross. A Swiss-born psychiatrist, she devoted her career to helping patients through the dying process after observing that the physicians she worked with were uncomfortable with their dying patients, and she was appalled when she witnessed that these patients were being left to die alone (Health n.d.).

In her first book, *On Death and Dying*, Dr. Kubler-Ross proposed that death be treated as a normal stage of life and that the dying patient be helped through understanding the five stages that the dying go through. The stages are: denial, anger, bargaining, depression, and acceptance, in no particular order. The dying may move in and out of the different stages, as they are not linear. The stages of death have also been applied to those who are struggling with grief after the loss of a loved one. Personally, I tend to believe that neither death nor grief can be limited to just five stages, but it is a place to start. The griever who is struggling with complicated grief typically becomes stuck in the first two stages of denial and anger, and struggles to find a way to move out of these first stages.

As an advocate for the dying, Kubler-Ross' work became the catalyst for the hospice movement, where the dying were moved from the acute patient setting to a palliative, homelike setting. She continued her work over the decades, determined to break through the layer of professional denial that kept patients from exploring and sharing their innermost concerns and feelings about death (Health n.d.).

Dying is an integral part of life, as natural and predictable as being born. But whereas birth is cause for celebration, death has become a dreaded and unspeakable issue to be avoided by every means possible in our modern society. Perhaps it is that in spite of all our technological advances. We may be able to delay it, but we cannot escape it. We, no less than other, non-rational animals, are destined to die at the end of our lives. And death strikes indiscriminately – it cares not at all for the status or position of the ones it chooses; everyone must die, whether rich or poor, famous or unknown. Even good deeds will not exclude their doers from the sentence of death; the good die as often as the bad. It is perhaps this inevitable and unpredictable quality that makes death so frightening to many people. Especially those who put a high value on being in control of their own existence are offended by the thought that they too are subject to the forces of death (D. E. Kubler-Ross, Death: The Final Stages of Growth 1975).

Towards the end of her life, Dr. Kubler-Ross expanded her work on death to address the spirituality involved in dying,

> Death is simply a shedding of the physical body like the butterfly shedding its cocoon. It is no different from taking off a suit of clothes one no longer needs. It is a transition to a higher state of consciousness where you continue to perceive, to understand, to laugh, and to be able to grow (D. E. Kubler-Ross, Life Lessons 2000).

ERNEST BECKER

Ernest Becker was an American cultural anthropologist who won a Pulitzer Prize in 1974 for his controversial book, *The Denial of Death*. In the book, he proposed that the basic motivation for human behavior is our biological need to control our anxiety surrounding our subconscious fear of death.

> Man is literally split in two: he has an awareness of his own splendid uniqueness in that he sticks out of nature with a towering majesty, and yet he goes back into the ground a few feet in order to blindly and dumbly rot and disappear forever. It is a terrifying dilemma to be in and to have to live with. The lower animals are, of course, spared this painful contradiction, as they lack a symbolic identity and the self-consciousness that goes with it. They merely act and move reflexively as they are driven by their instincts. If they pause at all, it is only a physical pause; inside they are anonymous, and even their faces have no name. They live in a world without time,

pulsating, as it were, in a state of dumb being. This is what has made it so simple to shoot down whole herds of buffalo or elephants. The animals don't know that death is happening and continue grazing placidly while others drop alongside them. The knowledge of death is reflective and conceptual, and animals are spared it. They live and they disappear with the same thoughtlessness: a few minutes of fear, a few seconds of anguish, and it is over. But to live a whole lifetime with the fate of death haunting one's dreams and even the most sun-filled days—that's something else (Becker 1973).

Becker's theory is that we are subconsciously terrified of our own mortality. This repressed fear taints every action we take during life, and as long as we seek to find meaning outside of ourselves, in the external world, we will ultimately fail. Meaning can be found only when we look within the self.

Becker proposes the concept of society as a symbolic hero system that allows the practice of "heroics" (Becker 1973). By fulfilling their role in a "hero-driven" society, or by pursuing and realizing extraordinary accomplishments, humans maintain a sense of self-esteem, which gives them a false sense of meaning in life (Ernest Becker Biography n.d.).

According to Becker when the fear of death is channeled properly, it can be a motivating force to propel individuals into phenomenal achievements with the goal that those achievements will transcend their physical mortality.

PHILIPPE ARIES

Aries was a French historian whose most prominent work was to study the history of the changes in Western attitudes towards death. Aries saw death as a social construction.

Aries' book, *The Hour of our Death*, covers the history of death over the last thousand years, and he specifically notes how death rituals were similar in all cultures up until the last century, when Western death rituals underwent significant changes. Aries argues that in our modern age, "there has been an 'abdication of the community' from death; death is left to an 'enormous mass of atomized individuals;' death has become an increasing solitary, almost 'invisible' phenomenon" (Nisbet 1981).

Aries wrote that the communal openness of dying and death in the Middle Ages gave death a "tamed" and concrete quality. He describes the changes in death over the last century as signifying a greater preoccupation with the general idea of mortality. Aries concludes, "This life in which death was removed to a prudent distance seems less loving of things and people than the life in which death was the center" (Nisbet 1981).

Aries describes a new type of dying in the twentieth century, one in which we sanitize, hospitalize, and hide death. The family is no longer providing the hands-on care for the dying or preparation for the burial, as they did in previous centuries. As we have handed these duties over to the medical community and funeral homes, we have distanced ourselves from the dying, hence creating two separate worlds, one for the living and one for the dying. Aries labels this modern period of death, "Forbidden, or wild death" (Aries 1982).

The impact of war on the American perspective on death

Modern warfare and the ability to kill or injure mass numbers of soldiers and civilians within a relatively short time has also influenced our American perspective on death over the last century and a half.

The American Civil War claimed the largest number of American casualties of any war, an estimated 618,000. One out of every five men deployed in the Civil War died, affecting a large percentage of families within the US. The casualty numbers were so enormous that neither the government nor the people were prepared to deal with the mass carnage. Bodies went unclaimed and unburied. Traditional burial rituals were bypassed (Waldman 2014).

World War I claimed 116,575 American casualties, and World War II claimed 405,399 (Waldman 2014). Since these casualties occurred overseas, families were unable to engage in their burial rituals and obtain closure surrounding the deaths of their loved ones.

According to sociologist John Stephenson, World War II is used to mark the shift that was seen in the American attitude towards death. Traditional and extensive mourning traditions and the sentimental approach to grief were suddenly seen as old-fashioned and a waste of time. It is proposed that the combined deaths in WWI and WWII produced a type of "death overload." The multiple losses that families experienced led to a desire to rid reality of extensive grieving and mourning rituals and seek out the good life, free from death and sorrow. A cultural shift began during this time in history, with a turning away from the traditional rites of grieving and from the messy reality of death (Stephenson n.d.).

Shifting our perspective on death

Man sacrifices his health to make money. Than he sacrifices his money to recuperate his health. Then he is so anxious about

the future that he does not enjoy the present; the result being that
he does not live in the present or the future; he lives as if he is
never going to die, and then dies having never really lived.

—DALAI LAMA

The time is now for a cultural shift within Western society. We begin by becoming more aware of how our fear of death affects our ability to live with more depth and more empathy as a society. The long-term goal is to transform into a society that has a healthier perspective on pain, illness, and death, which are natural parts of life. Our death-denying culture only makes the inevitable death of the physical body—the outcome for all of us—a more painful and isolating experience than it needs to be.

The shift can begin with us, each of us who has experienced the death of someone we love or who has personally confronted serious illness and consequently the awareness of mortality. We should not have to feel ashamed of our pain or be ostracized for it. We can share our experiences, thereby increasing others' awareness of our societal tendency towards denial and defiance of death. We can begin to pave a new path to a new cultural reality, where empathy, community, and acceptance can become our new norm.

The mustard seed

Parables are stories that contain words of wisdom to help us get through difficult times. At the peak of my struggle with my losses, I came across the Chinese parable of the mustard seed. The story had a significant effect on me and helped me recognize just how universal grief and loss are; even when we feel all alone in our grief journey, so many others are taking this journey, as well.

In the story, a woman's young son dies suddenly from an illness. She is despondent. Carrying her son's dead body throughout her village, she begs her neighbors to help her bring him back to life. None of them can help her, but she continues to roam the village, cradling her son and sobbing, inconsolable. The neighbors fear she is losing her mind. Finally, the village apothecary sends her to a wise man at the temple who may be able to help the woman deal with her grief.

Entering the temple, the mother desperately throws herself and her son's body at the feet of the wise man, begging for his help. She tells him he must bring her son back to her. The wise man tells her to go back to her village and gather mustard seeds from all of her neighbors who had *not* been touched by death. He said he would make a medicine with those mustard seeds that would bring her son back to life. Full of hope, the woman set off for the village, determined to find the mustard seeds that would save her son.

She went from door to door throughout the village. Her neighbors were happy to offer her mustard seeds, but she could not accept them because every family had experienced some personal loss of its own. Conversing with her neighbors as she searched for mustard seeds, she discovered that every home in her village had been touched by grief. Through this shared experience of loss, she came to realize that death is an unavoidable part of life, something we all must endure.

The wise man had shown her that sharing her pain and grief with others who were also experiencing losses had not only helped her neighbors cope with their losses, but eventually healed her own.

PART 3

The Alchemy of Grief

The Alchemy of Grief

Life, as you know, it stops when someone you love dies.
What was once an unending future filled with love and compan-
ionship suddenly—and against your will—becomes an uncer-
tain future with no instructions on how to navigate the fallout,
a future that is filled with overwhelming pain, confusion, and
loneliness.
This is not what you had planned.
You will wonder at the things that seemed important before your
loss —all the unnecessary things that once seemed essential to
your happiness. You will also wonder at all the important moments you took for granted.
Grief produces a kind of alchemy of the soul.
Before loss, the soul was entombed by all of the irrelevant demands and notions of the ego.
After loss, through flames of pain, all your material desires and
trivial needs fall away, exposed as meaningless.
As the nonessentials fall away, what is revealed is the raw magnifi-
cence and wisdom of your soul
and the profound purpose of living this physical experience.
Your soul has intrinsic knowledge of how to heal your broken
heart: Let anything needless be burnt away.
Once uncovered, your soul can guide you to a place where the
important things will shine through—love, compassion, and
connection.
It doesn't mean you won't suffer at times
or experience moments of grief, but you will be able to move
through those painful moments more quickly, and the tears will
eventually transform into joyful smiles as you remember your
loved one.

A part of the healing process is getting to a point where you can recognize how blessed and fortunate you were to have experienced such a life-changing love. That's when your memories will become treasures, treasures that are yours forever and can never be lost.
You will always be connected to your loved one.
The anguish of grief cannot happen without great love.
Sometimes the tears and smiles, heartbreak and joy
will happen all at once, and you'll understand
that this is the very essence of the meaning of life.
This is the alchemy of grief.

A Griever's Right to Choose Their Path

There is no one path that a griever should walk. There is not
even a right path. There is only your path.
As a griever, you are already walking a path
That you did not ask to be on.
Your loved one's death gutted the life path you were walking together and thrust you onto this unwanted and lonely path of grief
and loss, a path that appears to lead nowhere.
You are left alone to find a passage that will lead you out of the
darkness and back to a place where you can repair the pieces of
your heart and the fragments of your splintered life.
A griever has a right to choose the direction most healing to their
heart, even if others don't understand or agree.
We all grieve in our own way, in our own time,
with our own thoughts about God and our own personal beliefs.
Some grievers forge their own path, find their own solutions to
heal their grieving hearts.
Some prefer a well-traveled path laid out for them by others,
relying on methods and beliefs that have worked for other
grievers.
Both paths are valid.
Forge your own path or follow one that is already established.
This choice is the griever's alone to make.
You may start down one path and realize it is not right for you.
Listen to your heart. Your heart is your inner compass to guide
you when you need to change direction. Some of you will have to
walk many paths to finally arrive at the one that is meant for you.
As grievers, we share a common experience:
Pain and loss.
As grievers, we are all focused on the same goal:
Healing our broken hearts.

Society doesn't understand our pain or our choices.
And when we are judged to be grieving poorly
or to have chosen the wrong path,
we are only subjected to more pain.
Sometimes other grievers don't understand our path, either, and
that is especially difficult. As grievers, we should do our best to
support—and not judge—other grievers. We should be respectful
and tolerant of other grievers, whose path may be different from
our own.
There are many paths, all leading to the same destination:
Healing.
You may have a different God than mine. That is okay.
Your cultural perception of death and the afterlife may be different. That is okay.
Every griever is fighting a tough battle.
We may not understand someone else's path, but that is okay.
It is not our path to understand.
As a griever, you have rights.
You have the right to choose your individual path to healing.
The path is yours alone to walk. The choice is yours alone to
make.
Do not let anyone else block your path
with their version of how your grief should look,
how your faith in God should look, or how your beliefs should
look.
Don't let anyone stop you from walking your path.
The path to make it through grief is yours to choose
and yours to walk.
Stay the course.
Find your true north.

CHAPTER 10

The Search for my Spiritual Path

Not until we are lost do we begin to understand ourselves.

—Walt Whitman

Drowning in Complicated Grief

When you are stuck in complicated grief, you feel like you're in the middle of the ocean, drowning. You are desperate to keep your head above water, but it's hard; your arms and legs feel like concrete, and you are so very tired of struggling.

You wonder whether it would be easier to surrender to the waves and allow yourself to sink. But some primal instinct in you demands that your lungs receive the oxygen that will keep you alive. Then, too, a part of you knows that your lost loved one does not want you to give up. So, you continue on.

Nearby in boats are people who love and support you, but they are not sure that you need help, and if so, how to help. You don't understand why the people in the boats can't see that you need someone to pull you out of the water. Your supporters never fully comprehend the depth of your struggle or that they are witnessing the near drowning of someone they love.

Eventually, you understand that no lifeline is about to be thrown to you from the well-meaning but unaware supporters in the boats. You are on your own. Exhausted, you force yourself to keep your head up and continue treading, every movement and breath threatening to be your last. Unexpectedly, your mind offers a suggestion you have never before considered—is it possible that your panicked struggle may be what is dragging you under?

You decide to surrender, stop struggling, and turn over onto your back. That's when you make the incredible discovery that your body is buoyant. Some part of you knows how to stay afloat.

As you gently float on the surface of the water, your face turned towards the night sky, you notice for the first time since your grief began how brilliant it is, how full of luminous stars. In that moment, you realize you are not alone in your struggle, and that the stars symbolize a greater Cosmic Source that is there to guide and encourage you.

You also understand that your lost loved one is there in the stars, as well. You were never alone.

You continue floating, keeping your eyes on the majestic beauty of the stars, until you've regained the strength and clarity to figure out how to get yourself to shore.

The choice

You don't have a soul. You are a soul. You have a body.

—*C.S. Lewis*

There are practical tools that can be used to heal complicated grief, but in my experience, the ultimate healer is a spiritual evolution. Your soul intrinsically knows what you need to heal your heart.

When I was struggling to stay afloat, I finally realized that I had a choice, even though I didn't feel I did. (At the time, I believed I was a victim of circumstance and that life sucked. I hadn't asked for the death of my loved one.) Eventually I understood that I had a choice between two alternatives:

- I could stay stuck in pain, treading water, indefinitely.
- I could commit to doing the work required to get me safely back to the shore, where the pain was at least manageable.

Ultimately, the tools for healing are within your grasp, but the choice of whether to reach for them is solely yours to make. You may not be emotionally ready to commit, however you can start thinking about what it will take to get you through this.

One destination, many paths

Do not go where the path may lead, go instead where there is no path and leave a trail.

—Ralph Waldo Emerson

The loss of my loved ones caused a deep rift in my faith, a faith that already had been built on unsteady ground. I had become disillusioned with God and life. I was certain that life was nothing but a house of cards, and the cards were stacked against—not just me—but all of us. I considered people who believed that God would answer their prayers foolish. To my view, God was an entity who randomly decided whom amongst his children would be spared pain and suffering, leaving others to suffer and struggle on their own. I became quite the cynic. Grief gave me a new lens through which to view life, and skepticism became my spiritual default setting.

Despite these overwhelming doubts about the existence and divine nature of God, I was driven by a deep desire for answers about how this life and God thing worked and where I fit into it all. I began an arduous, intense, solitary quest, determined to find some spiritual answers in a form that made sense to me. It took years of self-reflection and searching to find answers that eventually helped me develop my spiritual path, a path that offered me a clearer and broader perspective on the guidance that is sometimes hidden within the world's pain and suffering.

During my years of contemplation, I began to understand the influence that my religious upbringing had on my perception of God, and that it contributed to my developing an underlying fear of Him. I also realized that through my career as a nurse caring for critically-ill children, the apathy that God seemed to have for these suffering children only increased my earlier suspicions that God was not fair. I now see how these experiences reinforced my negative concept of God, but I can also see that there were moments I had overlooked, moments that compelled me to look deeper into my shallow opinions of God. Unfortunately, it took a tremendous amount of personal pain before I was finally able to appreciate the underlying message of life, love, and joy that had always been there for me to see. God had been there all along. I was just looking in the wrong places.

CHAPTER 11

—◦—

Life Experiences and my Spiritual Evolution

Life can only be understood backwards, but it must be lived forwards.

—Soren Kierkegaard

Indoctrination of innocence

Before you speak to me about your religion, first show it to me in how you treat other people; before you tell me how much you love your God, show me in how much you love all His children; before you preach to me of your passion for your faith, teach me about it through your compassion for your neighbors. In the end, I'm not as interested in what you have to tell or sell as in how you choose to live and give. (Cory Booker@corybooker Facebook post, April 24, 2012).

Like most of us, I was born into my religion. I lived the first thirty-nine years of my life according to a set of religious rules and beliefs that had been established by other people. Because these people were experts on the subject of God and had access to a higher power than I, I was expected to accept this information as my truth. Sounds like a foolproof solution. Shouldn't it be easier to sit back and let someone else do the work for you and tell you what to believe?

Unfortunately, my independent and headstrong personality fought against the seeming oppression. After all, wasn't God the one who was responsible for giving me the ability to reason and reflect upon the meanings of life and the divine? It frustrated me that I wasn't allowed to use this same intellect to evaluate the beliefs I was being taught. I couldn't help but notice inconsistencies in the stories I was told, and if I voiced my concern, I was made to feel that I was wrong for having the question in the first place. Eventually, I lost any sense of certainty in these experts, which led to a subconscious suspicion of God, and this left me feeling disconnected from Him.

The Church in which I was raised has many beautiful and mystical teachings, but centuries of doctrine and dogma have hidden the initial message of love and oneness that Jesus taught. Unfortunately, I absorbed the subliminal message that, although God loved me, He was someone to be feared. My mistakes were being recorded. God had a set of rules He wanted me to follow, and I was to strive for perfection. The problem was, like most other humans, I was far from perfect. As a young girl, I could imagine God looking down, shaking His head, and saying, "What am I going to do with that dis-obedient and misbehaving Rhonda?" Maybe I was just more aware of my imperfections than other kids, because I had the uncomfortable feeling that God did not approve of me. Good grief! Didn't God have better things to do than micromanage my life? Sadly, at a young age, I came to the conclusion that I would never measure up to God's expectations.

Although my initial relationship with God got off to a shaky start, I was able to relate to this Jesus guy. He seemed like a genuinely loving person, and I liked hearing his message of hope and of loving your neighbor as yourself. Then, as I learned more about Jesus, I was distraught to hear about the pain and suffering he was forced to go through during the crucifixion. Why did he have to die for me and my sins? I knew I wasn't perfect, but was I really that awful? The guilt and confusion continued to pile up and my fear of God grew. How could a loving father send his son to earth to go through all that pain and suffering? If He allowed that to happen to His own son, what would He allow to happen to me? It was a bit of a dilemma for me. I was supposed to love God, but instead, I had a swirl of conflicting emotions that no one else seemed to have. I thought God was a big, overbearing, and uncaring jerk. (Insert lightning bolt here.) What was wrong with me? Surely I was headed to hell, or at the very least, purgatory. Frankly, I was okay with that possibility. The thought of living eternity with such a judgmental being was not appealing.

Eventually, I just accepted that God was going to be disappointed in me, but I was also a little disillusioned and disappointed in Him, as well.

Through the eyes of a pediatric nurse: Finding meaning in life's injustices

A statue stands in a shaded place
an angel girl with an upturned face
a name is written on a polished rock
a broken heart that the world forgot.

—Martina McBride, "Concrete Angel"

In my early twenties, I felt a strong calling to become a nurse. I knew that I wanted to take care of children, and I spent eleven years as a pediatric intensive care nurse. This calling was a double-edged sword for me. The opportunity to use my skills to help heal children who were sick and suffering was one of the most rewarding experiences of my life, and my career developed into a genuine vocation. Yet, the work also exposed me to a harsh reality: that the youngest and most undeserving in our society, children—who should have had their entire lives ahead of them—die, and sometimes they die under unimaginable circumstances. I witnessed the full potential of human cruelty intentionally inflicted against those who were unable to protect themselves. The pediatric intensive care unit (PICU) officially introduced me to the dark side of human nature. Child abuse became my greatest enemy. As witness to these horrors, I questioned the character of God once again. How could a supposedly loving God allow such tragedy and injustice to happen to the most innocent and untarnished members of society, our children? His children.

Witnessing this abuse brought up the unresolved and subconscious fears of God that I had experienced as a child. If God was truly good, how could He allow this to happen to these innocent and trusting souls? Despite my fears, I still found myself praying to God on behalf of these children while I cared for their broken bodies. Prayer that should have brought me comfort brought me confusion instead, and more unanswered questions. Could God not see when His children needed help without us praying to Him? To me, this was equivalent to having to convince a lifeguard to do his job and save someone who was drowning. The lifeguard has a better view than we do. He knows exactly what is happening to this drowning child. What was the problem? I really didn't understand.

I saw children who had suffered atrocious abuse and seemed to have no one who truly cared for them. Even if they survived their injuries, their futures would be very difficult. Where was God when these children needed Him? I was indignant. Again, why would a loving and all-knowing God need to be begged to help a suffering child? I came to believe it was possible that God was a heartless and indifferent brute (lightning strike again) who sat up in the sky deciding who deserved His help and who didn't. My heart broke for the children He seemed to have forgotten.

I eventually left the PICU because the sorrow and anger I experienced when another abused child rolled through the doors required more energy and heart than I was able to continue giving. I could not tolerate seeing *one more broken child.* It was the same scenario every time, with new names and faces. While caring for the abused children, I couldn't stop imagining the torment and fear they must have endured to receive the injuries I saw. How could God be witness to these abominations and do nothing to stop them?

After leaving the PICU, I discovered that I couldn't forget the traumatic and many times fatal injuries that these children received—and from someone who was supposed to love and protect them. Their precious faces and names will always haunt me. I felt compelled to do what I had hoped God would do—to try to find a way to protect as many of these children as possible. This led me to another calling, volunteering to help prevent child abuse within my community.

Years later, after overcoming my anger and fear of God, I came to understand that this calling to prevent child abuse was just one of many ways that God works behind the scenes. I believe that I was intentionally being used as an instrument to help keep these children safe. And just maybe, my initial calling to work in the field of pediatric intensive care nursing was not random, either. Perhaps I was purposely called to bear witness to the injustices I had experienced, which motivated me to do something to help prevent them.

We need to notice these little Aha moments. I believe these intuitions are just a few of the ways God communicates with us and tries to create change in the world. Albert Einstein, who I believe was a mystic and who was one of the greatest theoretical physicists of all time, said, "Coincidence is God's way of remaining anonymous."

Loss of faith or search for truth?

Reality is merely an illusion, albeit a persistent one.

—ALBERT EINSTEIN

The Universe is wider than our views of it

—HENRY DAVID THOREAU

After personal crisis entered my life, my religious beliefs did not provide adequate answers for me. I discovered that before beginning my search for answers, I first needed to empty my cup of my established belief system. When you have been raised with one set of beliefs, it is quite a challenge even to be able to read new information without seeing it through the filter of your old beliefs. It took years of work for me to unlearn all of my beliefs and fears about God and to open myself up to all of the possibilities that God and the universe hold.

There is an old Zen story about a master who was attempting to explain something new to his student. The master was unable to get his message across because the student was full of biased notions about the way life worked and was not able to hear what the master was trying to teach. The master lifted the teapot to pour tea into the student's cup, which had already been full and was now running over. The student exclaimed, "Master, you cannot fill my cup when it is already full!"

The master replied, "Yes, you must first empty your cup of your preconceived notions and thoughts about life to make room for the truths that I am trying to teach you" (Ross n.d.).

During my search, I found teachings ascribed to Jesus that are not taught in today's Church, and these painted a much broader picture of his life for me. These teachings emphasize how Jesus wanted us to live, how we were to treat others, and his eventual transcendence of it all—not on his suffering and crucifixion due to our sinful nature. These teachings resonated with me because they expanded on what I felt were the most important messages of Jesus' ministry—love, forgiveness, and the resurrection, rather than on his extensive suffering that the Church tells us was due to our sinful nature. I was ready to shed the years of guilt, shame, and conformity that I had absorbed because of what I now believed were misinterpretations of Jesus' message by the Church.

The search

After looking into the history of my own religion, I also examined several of the world's major religions, and found that I was fascinated with the mystics. I found many parallel teachings within the core of all major religions: Christianity, Judaism, Buddhism, Islam, and Hinduism.

The mystics believed that direct knowledge of God and spiritual truths can be obtained through subjective experience. Mystical teachings are at the core of almost all of today's religious traditions. These ancient teachings are hidden within the religious texts and are responsible for the modern contemplative practices that provide a direct mode of communion with the Divine. These practices allow for the individual spiritual seeker to "know" God without going through external religious sources for the experience.

Down the theoretical rabbit hole

> *The religion of the future will be a cosmic religion. It should transcend a personal God and avoid dogma and theology. Covering both the natural and the spiritual, it should be based on a religious sense arising from the experience of all things natural and spiritual as a meaningful unity.*

> —ALBERT EINSTEIN

I'm going to make a 180-degree turn now and talk a bit about modern-day science and the study of quantum physics, as well as the role quantum physics is inadvertently playing to prove what the mystics proposed millennia ago. Quantum physics is the theoretical basis of modern physics that explains the nature and behavior of matter and energy on the atomic and subatomic levels (Rouse 2015).

According to scientific and theoretical physicists, everything we see is energy that is given life by consciousness. Despite what our eyes tell us, there is nothing truly solid within the universe—including our bodies; there is only energy that is constantly vibrating at different frequencies. And most amazing of all, that energy can never die. Scientists are discovering that what we view as physical reality is actually an illusion; it only appears to be real when there is an observer to witness it. That rock over yonder? Nothing but molecules, atoms, and subatomic particles made mostly of air, vibrating at a slow enough frequency that it appears solid (Bancarz 2015).

Science is making great strides in the theory of consciousness (what gives us subjective experience) and is coming to the conclusion that, without consciousness, nothing in the universe would exist (Bancarz 2015). Max Planck, Nobel Prize winning originator of quantum theory, suggested, "I regard consciousness as fundamental. I regard matter as derivative from consciousness. We cannot get behind consciousness. Everything that we talk about, everything that we regard as existing, postulates consciousness" (Planck 1931).

I am certainly not a scientist and don't claim to be an expert on what is happening in the field of consciousness and theoretical metaphysics, but as a medical professional and as someone who believes there is more to this universe than what we believe we are seeing, I find it fascinating. I believe that science is proving that there is a Creator/Source/God, whatever you would like to call it, infusing life into matter and making everything we see a reality. Scientific and religious mystics believe that consciousness is a direct extension of God and that this consciousness infuses life into everything we see. Some people think that the terms *mind* and *consciousness* are synonymous.

Albert Einstein had the vision to see that space and time are compressible. Through his vision, he created a different way of viewing the universe based on understanding that what appears to be "solid" matter is really just energy. Einstein said, "The most beautiful emotion we can experience is the mystical. It is the power of all true art and science. He to whom this emotion is a stranger, who can no longer wonder and stand rapt in awe, is as good as dead." He also stated that, "Religion without science is blind, and science without religion is lame" (Waters n.d.).

Niels Bohr, a Danish physicist who won the Nobel Peace Prize for his work surrounding atomic and quantum theory, stated, "Everything we call real is made of things that cannot be regarded as real. If quantum physics hasn't profoundly shocked you yet, you don't understand it" (Palermo 2013). Even the scientists are stunned at what they're discovering at the quantum level and what these discoveries are telling us, not only about the universe, but about the very essence of what gives us life.

Einstein wrote to the family of a recently deceased friend: "Now he has departed from this strange world a little ahead of me. That means nothing. People like us, who believe in physics, know that the distinction between past, present and future is only a stubbornly persistent illusion" (Clark 2013).

Realizing that there is more to this life than what we can see and that a part of us can never die had a positive effect on my ability to heal my grief. My husband and son weren't dead; they had just changed form. They were now spirit. And within this body, I am also spirit, which means that my loved ones and I will always be together. I believe that spirit transcends the physical world. Spirit and love are interchangeable, and neither of them can ever be lost.

CHAPTER 12

How a Medium Helped Me Navigate Grief

Life and death are one thread, the same line viewed from two different sides.

—*Lao Tzu*

As you read about my personal experiences of connecting with my loved ones through a medium after they died, I hope that you can for a moment set aside any preconceived notions you might have about how this life and death thing works. My wish is that anyone who has known the pain of losing someone they love might have the chance to experience the peace of mind I received upon having confirmation that my lost loved ones were safe and had moved on to another spiritual realm.

As you suspend your beliefs for just a few moments, I ask that you allow your mind to be open to the vast realm of possibilities. You may find that your concept of God and the universe begins to expand, and some of the mysteries about life and death may be revealed to you.

Modern-day science is inadvertently proving what the mystics proposed millennia ago. What we are learning about the universe can be considered a type of rebirth of ancient philosophical wisdom. Everything we see, our loved ones, our planet, our universe—all of it is energy that has been given life by consciousness. Consciousness is a direct extension of God.

Despite what our eyes tell us, there is nothing truly solid within the universe—including our bodies. There is only energy that vibrates at different frequencies. Most amazing of all, the energy that creates everything we see can never die. You? Me? Our lost loved ones? At the very core of each of us we are nothing but energy, which means that a part of us never dies. Our energy goes on after physical death. Ultimately, energy is energy, whether it resides in subatomic particles that seem to form a body or in its original state as energy existing as spirit.

Considering all of this information, why would we be surprised that there are people, or minds, that can connect with this energy and transcend the divide between what we view as the "living" and the "dead?" If you allow it to, death can open your eyes to the transient and mysterious nature of life like nothing else can. As Shakespeare so wisely said, "There are more things in heaven and earth than are dreamt of in your philosophy."

Where did my loved one go?

It's not what you look at that matters, it's what you see.

—WALT WHITMAN

After my late husband died, along with the shock and pain, I was also confused. Steve was young, healthy, and vibrant when he died at the age of forty-six. I couldn't comprehend how someone so dynamic, someone who absolutely exuded life, could suddenly be gone. Exactly where did "Steve" go after he died? I knew some part of him continued on. I understood that his body was gone, but I still felt his spirit.

I seemed to be receiving signs that Steve was still with us. One night, when all of the older kids were out of the house, I put Maggie, who was two years old and still in her baby bed, to sleep. Her room was upstairs, and I had a baby monitor so I could hear her if she needed me. She was a very good sleeper, and just as she typically did, she slept through the night. But when I went up to get her in the morning, her rocking chair, which was always in the far corner of her room twelve feet away from the baby bed, had been pulled up close to it, as if someone had been watching her sleep. Steve used to read to her, feed her, and rock her to sleep in that rocking chair. I had the uncanny feeling that he had somehow found a way to spend time in that rocking chair to watch her sleep.

My bedroom was right off the stairs, and I also heard footsteps coming down the stairs from Maggie's room at night when no one else was home. I'm not talking one or two footsteps, I heard someone come down the entire flight of stairs. Was it my imagination? Was it hopeful thinking? I didn't know.

Other little things happened. When my sister-in-law was over checking on me and we started talking about Steve, a lamp turned on all by itself. This was a twist-switch lamp that actually was difficult to twist off and on, even when you were trying. How was it possible that it turned on by itself? My sister-in-law and I both felt that Steve was in the room with us and had found a way to communicate.

I understood that Steve was physically dead, but why did I still feel him around me? The sense that more was happening and that

Steve was still with us consumed me. I began reading anything I could find on life after death and near-death experiences. I was fascinated to understand what Steve had gone through and what he might be doing at this point on the "other side."

While I did find some answers to my questions, what I ultimately discovered is that death forever changes the way you look at life. I became willing to open my mind to the possibility that life was not as simple as I had believed. I started to understand that so much more is going on than just what we experience with our five senses.

I understand if you are initially skeptical. At the time of Steve's death, I'd had no experience with psychics or mediums, and because of my religious upbringing, I did not believe in them. But once again, I urge you to keep an open mind as I share my story with you. The truth is, if someone had told me ten years ago that a pair of dirty socks would prove to me that there is no death and that my lost loved one lived on, I wouldn't have believed them, either.

Through the looking glass

Six months after Steve died, a friend whose husband had died in the same airplane accident as Steve called me. My friend shared with me that when she had been visiting her family in Iowa, they had urged her to talk with a well-known medium in the area who was trusted for her abilities. The medium's name was Moriah Rhame.

My friend followed her family's advice and talked with Moriah. During the reading that connected my friend to her husband, Steve had popped into her reading and asked her to give me the message that he wanted to talk to me through Moriah.

I was speechless. My late-husband was sending a message that he wanted to talk to me? I had never really thought about communicating with a medium before. But to hear that Steve was asking to talk to me was too great a temptation to deny. Was it possible I could actually talk with him?

I was suffering terribly without Steve. I hadn't moved on at all in the six months since his death. In fact, I still had all of his clothing and personal items, and they were in exactly the same places they were when he died, as if any day he would come walking back in the door, ready to resume life as the head of our family.

Steve had a habit of leaving his dress socks hanging from his dress shoes in the closet so that he could use them a second day. This is how they were when he died, and six months later the first thing I saw every day as I entered our closet were his dirty socks hanging out of his shoes.

When I did finally call Moriah, I was a bit skeptical. I imagined she would have generic things to say to me...like, "You have pictures of him all over your house. You are still wearing his ring." I thought she would have to ask me questions about him before she could give me any information. But what actually happened was beyond anything I had imagined or hoped for.

Moriah immediately started talking to me about what information she was seeing and receiving. She told me that this guy who was in front of her was funny (Steve was hilarious), and she went on to accurately physically describe him. There were times she was talking to me, and then she would start talking to him. I wasn't sure what was happening.

One minute into the conversation, however, what she said made me catch my breath. Moriah asked me, "Why is he laughing and telling me something about socks?" At the mention of socks, I immediately sat up and paid very close attention. *No one* knew I still had Steve's dirty socks hanging in our closet, not even my family or closest friends.

Moriah continued. "Yes, he's laughing and telling me that he can't believe you saved his dirty socks, and it's a good thing he didn't leave out his dirty underwear or you would have saved those, too!" I was speechless. That is exactly what Steve would have said to me.

At that moment, I knew Moriah was somehow connecting with my late husband and that some part of Steve had survived his physical death. He was still the same loving, funny man I knew, and he seemed to have retained his dry sense of humor. Just as in our physical life, he was able to make me laugh when I was talking to him through Moriah. He also told me that he was still flying airplanes on the other side, but that over there, "the sky was *not* the limit."

My grandmother, Agnes, who had died in 1992, also came through during this first reading. We had been very close, and when I was struggling through hard times, I often thought of her and asked her for strength, which I always felt I received. Moriah told me that an older, tall woman wearing a pantsuit was holding out a peony for me (my grandmother's favorite flower), and that she was still with me.

Steve wanted me to know that he was very worried about my physical health. He warned me that I had to start taking better care of myself or I would get sick. Moriah told me that he said he was sending me a white flower to remind me of his love. Just a few weeks later, I had an episode of internal bleeding (I was on anticoagulants and experienced complications), and I was hospitalized for several days and required multiple transfusions.

After I recovered and went back home, Steve's parents sent me a dozen multi-colored roses. Two of them were white. Within a week every rose had died, but one white rose remained as beautiful as it was the first day and it stayed that way for *three weeks*. Twenty-one days after I received the white rose, it looked as fresh and alive as it had on the first day. I had no doubt that this was the white flower Steve had said he would send me.

When I talked with Moriah a couple of weeks after my recovery, Steve told me that he had been with me the entire time I was in the hospital; he was worried that I could pass to the other side. He confirmed that the white rose I had received was the reminder that he was with me, and he was sending me his love.

Steve also tried to warn me about the seriousness of the self-destructive behavior that was occurring with my children, Kathryn and Jordan, before I even saw any of the warning signs. He gave me many suggestions for how to help them, from sending them out-of-state to camps for teens, to career suggestions to keep them busy and out of trouble, to not allowing them to be around their biological father, who was toxic to them. He had so many suggestions, but even with his warnings and advice for handling their issues, in the end, I didn't fully grasp the gravity of the situation, and I was too late to change their paths.

Steve also did not have a will when he died and left quite a mess for me to sort out. Through Moriah, he told me about what pitfalls I should expect to go through and how I should deal with several very sensitive family situations and what I could expect to happen. He was spot-on with all of his information.

Honestly, I experienced so many amazing experiences talking with Steve through Moriah that it's hard to limit the story to just a few. The last experience I will share with you is when Steve played matchmaker because he didn't want me to be alone.

Around a year after Steve died, he started saying that I was too young to be alone and he wanted me to have a partner who could help me raise Maggie and help with my older children. He went on to tell me that I had another soulmate out there. Moriah described that Steve was showing her the symbol for the "scales and balances," and she thought Steve was indicating something about the legal system. She then said she was seeing Washington (I wrongly assumed she meant Washington State). She also said she was seeing that our relationship (this other soulmate and me) would begin over the internet.

Well, that was all good, but we had absolutely no idea what to do with this information. Who was this guy? And where was I supposed to find him? We didn't have a clue. But that didn't stop Steve. I talked with Moriah once a month at that point, and Steve constantly reminded us that we needed to be looking for this guy.

A few months later, Moriah got a sudden feeling that I was supposed to go on eHarmony.com to find this guy that Steve wouldn't give up on. I hadn't done any dating, real-life or internet, but what could it hurt? I signed up for eHarmony that day. That same day, I was matched up with numerous potential suitors. I was drawn to one of them right away. His name was Michael.

Long story short: Michael lived in Washington DC, worked for the FBI, and was an incredible man. We went on to have a relationship on the internet. We have now been married seven years. You can imagine that I felt I had Steve's approval to remarry, because he is the one who set Michael and me up in the first place).

I'm not sharing this story with you to recommend Moriah as a matchmaker; I share it with you to clarify that I don't believe there is any way that the experiences I had with her could have come from any other source than Steve.

I think Steve knew about all of the future heartache that was in store for me with the impending death of my son, and all of the health complications I was going to experience, and he didn't want me to go through them alone.

If you are wondering whether remarrying made the grieving process easier, I can tell you that the answer is a resounding No. Grief doesn't stop or go away for anyone or anything. It may hang out in the background for a while, but there is no escaping it. And there is no replacing someone who meant the world to you, even if you find someone else who means the world to you. The loss of your loved one will always leave an unfillable void in your heart.

I am blessed and so very grateful that I had Michael by my side as I walked my grief path and that he has been such a loving father to Maggie. But it was very hard on him to see me go through so much pain when there was really no way he could help me. Ultimately, I alone had to do the work to learn how to carry my grief and to get myself to a place where I was able to find some joy in life again.

A mother's panic

To lose a child is to lose a piece of yourself.

—Dr. Burton Grebin

On August 26, 2008, my son Jordan died of kidney failure. He had been sick most of his life. I thought I was prepared for the inevitability that he would die young. But I wasn't prepared. Not even close. I was devastated. I knew I had to talk with Jordan right away. My mother's heart had to know that my child was okay.

I talked with Moriah the day after Jordan died. Moriah described for me what Jordan had seen in his hospice room as he died. He had seen me, his grandmother, his sisters, and his extended family all sobbing at his bedside. He said he knew that we loved him, but until he saw the depth of our pain he hadn't truly understood how deep our love for him was. He made it very clear that he didn't want us to be so sad and that he was still with us. He also wanted Moriah to tell me that not only was he free of pain now, but he could also have all of the Doritos and Mountain Dew (his favorite food and drink) that he desired. He was in his own personal heaven.

Although I still had a long road of grief to travel to recover from the loss of my son, the relief I experienced when I was able to talk with him and know that he was safe is indescribable.

I've gone on to talk to my loved ones through Moriah about once a year over the past several years. Steve is harder for Moriah to access now, but she is still able to connect to Jordan. It is remarkable to me how much he has grown spiritually on the other side. My son now provides guidance to me and advice to pass on to his siblings about what is happening in all of our lives.

⌣⃗

Moriah has become someone I consider a dear friend. It is obvious to me that Moriah feels an obligation to use her skills and gifts as a medium to help those who have lost someone they love. For her, being a medium is not a job; it is a calling. She is a mother of four and does philanthropic work in her community. She is an upstanding person and an amazing and trustworthy medium.

I encourage you to do your research before you choose a medium. Moriah is the real deal, but there are mediums out there who take advantage of people who are grieving.

You can find more information on Moriah at her website: www. moriahthemedium.com.

CHAPTER 13

Your Spiritual Search

True wisdom comes to each of us when we realize how little we understand about life, ourselves, and the world around us.

—*SOCRATES*

Not until we are lost do we begin to understand ourselves.

—*HENRY DAVID THOREAU*

YOU MAY BE wondering what spiritual evolution has to do with healing grief. In my experience, unless you have an established spiritual or religious foundation in which you are confident, it is essential that you at least consider the possibility that there is a spiritual path out there waiting for you to discover it. Your personal spiritual path can be used as a light to guide you through the dark days of grief and eventually to assist in bringing you out on the other side.

Some of you will find peace of mind in religious or spiritual traditions that have been passed down through your family. Some of you will not fit so easily into these prefabricated forms and will feel unsatisfied with what you have been taught to believe. When you fall into this second category, life frequently provides opportunities to shake up your former beliefs and urge you out of your comfort zone, enabling you to find the path that is meant specifically for you. This last section of the book was written for these seekers.

Whether you have already found your spiritual path or are just starting out on your spiritual quest, I believe it is essential for all to show mutual respect for our fellow human beings' beliefs and respective spiritual journeys. Many paths lead to the same destination—God and our higher selves. Contrary to popular belief, there is no one path that has the monopoly on God. Precious time and energy are wasted when we feel the need to point out what we believe is wrong with other spiritual and religious paths. I believe this is one of the meanings that can be taken from Jesus' teaching from Matthew 7:3, "Why do you notice the speck of sawdust in your brother's eye, but pay no attention to the plank in your own eye?" Our focus should be on fortifying our own path while being tolerant of those whose beliefs are different from ours. It is even possible that we can learn from others' paths and utilize this knowledge to expand on our own beliefs.

Upon discovering the path meant for you, you will come across the healing balm that can be used to soothe the many wounds that life has dealt you. Ultimately, your spiritual path will give you a greater understanding of yourself and your purpose in life, as well as greater empathy and love for your fellow man.

While searching for my path, initially my grief seemed to intensify. I was plunged into a new depth of anguish, where a profound personal spiritual fire was lit under me. This spiritual fire eventually provided experiences that exposed and revealed some of the mysteries of life. I believe this is what Jesus was referring to when he said, "And so I tell you, keep on asking, and you will receive what you ask for. Keep on seeking, and you will find. Keep on knocking, and the door will be opened to you. For everyone who asks, receives. Everyone who seeks, finds. And to everyone who knocks, the door will be opened (Luke 11:9-10).

Through these spiritual encounters that I believe were ignited by pain, I came to understand that ultimately every one of us is here voluntarily to participate in this dualistic experience called human life. We come into the body as spirits, knowing that at times life will be like a crap shoot, generating random things both good and bad that we have no control over. This is an inescapable part of human life; it is part of the deal we accept when we come into a body. We are here to experience a world of "opposites," pain as well as joy. Being in a physical body provides us the experience of many different forms of love: parental love, platonic love, intimate and sexual love, sibling love, and love of your fellow man. Along with all these different forms of human love, we also experience the opposite of love: fear. Experiencing all the emotions related to fear fosters more appreciation of the joy and love in life, which ultimately are our eternal nature.

The purpose of pain, if we allow it, can be to make us more empathetic to others; it opens our eyes to the connection we all share. Pain brings you to a fork in the road where you have to choose between two distinct directions: hope and despair. Despair is an easy choice, but a stagnant one that leads to a dead end. Hope is more difficult to choose because it requires more work, but the work will reward you with a new perspective on life. Fighting the inevitable, or believing that we are victims of circumstance, only keeps us living in a state of confusion about the greater purpose of life that can be found when we look deeper into the mysteries of what adversity has to reveal.

Love is the substance that connects us all. When we understand this concept, we automatically start living as if we and our neighbors, even those we secretly despise, really are one. Within each of us is a spirit so divine, so luminously exquisite, that words cannot provide an adequate description. Ultimately, in our spiritual state, each of us is made of light and love, and we know only joy.

> *To see a world in a grain of sand and heaven in a wild flower.*
> *Hold infinity in the palms of your hand and eternity in an hour.*

—William Blake

How do I start my search?

> *Life unfolds itself in mysterious ways.*

—KAHLIL GIBRAN

- **What do you currently believe?** Do your beliefs help you through the experience of losing someone you love, or do they cause you more pain and confusion? If your beliefs do not help you deal with the loss of your loved one, you may not be on the right spiritual path. Your personal spiritual path may be out there waiting for you to find.
  (I want to note that if you are happy with your spiritual or religious path and teachings and your path is providing answers and comfort for you, then you are right where you need to be. There is no reason to read on. The following information is for those who have unanswered questions or who do not find comfort and resonance in their current path.)

- **What unanswered questions do you have about death, life, and God?** You will find that your questions about what happens after death lead to deeper and deeper questions about the meaning of life and why we are here. These questions will help you as you start your search.
- **Read. Research. Resonate.** Discover what resonates with you, whether Eastern philosophy, New Age theories, near-death experiences, or a major religion. If they reverberate within you, explore one or many spiritual teachers/paths as stepping stones while you develop your spiritual path. Maybe one specific religion or path is right for you. However, it is possible that several teachers can contribute to making a foundation for your personal spiritual path.

Spiritual teachers and teachings that helped me find my spiritual path

MYSTICS OF ALL RELIGIONS

Mystical teachings are at the core of almost all of today's religious traditions. These ancient teachings are "hidden" within the religious texts and are responsible for the modern contemplative practices that provide a direct mode of communion with the Divine. These practices allow for the individual spiritual seeker to "know" God without going through external religious sources for the experience.

CORE/PARALLEL TEACHINGS OF MAJOR RELIGIONS

Christianity, Judaism, Hinduism, Islam, and Buddhism. All of the major world religions share the same root. Millennia of doctrine and dogma generated by religious leaders and politicians have shrouded the basic message of these religions. Remove the creed on the surface and you will find more similarities at the core than there are differences.

Take into consideration the most universal religious rule of all, The Golden Rule, as it is interpreted in these five religions (The Universality of the Golden Rule in World Religions 2016):

Christianity - All things whatsoever ye would that men should do to you, do ye so to them; for this is the law and the prophets (Matthew 7:1).

Buddhism - Hurt not others in ways that you yourself would find hurtful (Udana-Varga 5, 1).

Hinduism - This is the sum of duty; do naught onto others what you would not have them do unto you (Mahabharata 5, 1517).

Islam - No one of you is a believer until he desires for his brother that which he desires for himself (a Sunnah of Prophet Muhammad).

Judaism - What is hateful to you, do not do to your fellowman. This is the entire Law; all the rest is commentary (Talmud, Shabbat 3id).

A great book that describes the common root of the major religions is *The Wisdom Tree – A Journey to the Heart of God,* by Gary D. Guthrie. Guthrie describes that, "each religious or spiritual 'window' onto the experience of spirituality is like an individual lens that focuses a little differently. While none of them have the complete answer or the aim of life, they act more like fingers pointing to the core of God's love and to the inner circle of God's presence within us" (Guthrie 1997).

Books and authors that ignited my spiritual evolution

Alexander, Eben, *Proof of Heaven*

Cayce, Edgar, *Story of the Soul*

Chodron, Pema, *Living Beautifully with Uncertainty and Change*

Dyer, Wayne, *Change Your Thoughts, Change Your Life*

Einstein, Albert, *The World As I See It*

Foundation for Inner Peace, *A Course in Miracles*

Frankl, Victor E., *Man's Search for Meaning*

Guthrie, Gary D., *The Wisdom Tree – A Journey to the Heart of God*

Hawkins, David, *Power vs. Force*

Huxley, Aldous, *The Perennial Philosophy*

Kalinthi, Paul, *When Breath becomes Air*

Katie, Byron, *Loving What Is*

Kubler-Ross, Elisabeth, *On Life after Death, Life Lessons*

Medhus, Elisa, *My Son and the Afterlife: Conversations from the Other Side*

Merton, Thomas, *Mystics and Zen Masters*

Moody, Raymond, *Life After Life*

Moorjani, Anita, *Dying to Be Me: My Journey from Cancer, to Near Death, to True Healing*

Pagels, Elaine, *The Gnostics Gospel*

Ruiz, Don Miguel, *The Four Agreements*

Singer, Michael, *The Untethered Soul*

Tolle, Eckhart, *A New Earth*

Satori, Penny, *The Wisdom of Near-Death Experiences*

Smith, James Bryan, *Room of Marvels*

Walsch, Neale Donald, *The Storm before the Calm*

Weiss, Brian, *Many Lives, Many Masters*

Williamson, Marianne, *A Return to Love*

Zukav, Gary, *The Seat of the Soul*

Making the most of this thing called life

She was no longer wrestling with the grief, but could sit down with it as a lasting companion and make it a sharer in her thoughts.

—GEORGE ELIOT

Making the Most of This Thing Called Life
Time is such a strange thing after someone you love has died.
One day without my loved ones felt as long as ten years.
Ten years without them now feels like a lifetime.
Time seemed to almost stop
When I was trying to learn how to live without them.
After millions of steps on my grief journey, I finally realize that
Every step I take is a step closer to being with my loved ones
again.
I also realize that it is my choice whether to take these steps
With sorrow, or whether to find joy in the remainder of my
journey.
One day, sooner rather than later, we will see our loved ones
again.
Walk in joy or in sorrow.
The distance to your loved one is the same.
The choice is yours.

As I end this book, I am happy to report that a decade after the loss of my loved ones, although it has been an arduous journey, I have finally managed to find some peace and enjoyment in my scar-covered, but purpose-filled life, and I intend do my best to live my life to the fullest for the time I have remaining. I strongly believe that this is what Steve and Jordan would want for me.

I hope that through reading about how I found purpose in my life again, you will feel encouraged as you walk your path. You, too, can find a way to heal your life and gain some happiness. This is what your lost loved one would want for you as well.

Sending each of you strength on your journey,

Rhonda

When you are sorrowful look again in your heart,
and you shall see that in truth you are weep-
ing for that which has been your delight.

—KAHLIL GIBRAN

Bibliography

Aries, Philippe. *The Hour of Our Death: The Classic History of Western Attitudes Towards Death Over the Last One Thousand Years.* Vintage Books, 1982.

Badger, Madonna. "The Long Road Back: How to keep going after the unimaginable happens." November 13, 2013. http://www.vogue.com/865184/the-long-road-back-madonna-badger/.

Bancarz, Steven. "Proof that Consciousness Creates Reality." *Spirit Science.* April 5, 2015. http://thespiritscience.net/2015/04/05/proof-that-consciousness-creates-reality-welcome-to-the-matrix/.

Becker, Ernest. *The Denial of Death.* 1973.

Brody, Jane E. "When Grief Won't Relent." *The New York Times,* February 16, 2015.

Clark, Douglas. "Einstein and Michele Besso." *Quoting Einstein.* June 27, 2013. http://quotingeinstein.blogspot.com/2013/06/einstein-and-michele-besso.html.

Collier, Lorna. "Why We Cry." *American Psychological Association,* February 2014: 47.

Corona, Vicki. *Tahitian Choreographies.* 1989.

Ecology Global Network. *http://www.ecology.com/birth-death-rates/.* http://www.ecology.com/birth-death-rates/.

Ernest Becker Biography. http://www.deathreference.com/A-Bi/ Becker-Ernest.html#ixzz46NVvkGMg.

Gire, James T. "How Death Imitates Life: Cultural Influences on Conceptions of Death and Dying." *Online Readings in Psychology and Culture, Unit 14, Chapter 2.* http://www.wwu.edu/culture/ gire.htm.

Graham, Judith. "Grief can become so deep that life becomes paralyzed." *Chicago Tribune,* June 4, 2015.

Grief Intensity Scale. http://endoflife.weill.cornell.edu/research/ grief-intensity-scale.

Guthrie, Gary D. "The Gifts of Wisdom." In *The Wisdom Tree - A Journey to the Heart of God,* by Gary D. Guthrie, 139. Ocean Tree Books, 1997.

Harvard Health Publications, Harvard Medical School. March 2011. http://www.health.harvard.edu/staying-healthy/ understanding-the-stress-response.

Health, National Institute of. *Changing the Face of Medicine - Biography Dr. Elisabeth Kubler-Ross.* https://www.nlm.nih.gov/changingth-efaceofmedicine/physicians/biography_189.html.

"Inventory for Complicated Grief." *American Psychological Association.*

Joubert, Irma. *The Girl from the Train,* by Irma Joubert, 254. Thomas Nelson, 2015.

Mayo Clinic, Healthy Life Style, Stress Management, April 21, 2016, by Mayo Clinic Staff, http://www.mayoclinic. org/healthy-lifestyle/stress-management/in-depth/stress/ art-20046037.

Kubler-Ross, Elisabeth. *Death: The Final Stage of Growth.* 1975.

Nisbet, Robert. "Death in the West." *The New York Times*, February 22, 1981.

Online, Catholic. *St. Gianna Beretta Molla.* http://www.catholic. org/saints/saint.php?saint_id=6985.

Orloff, Dr. Judith. *The Health Benefit of Tears.* 2011. http://www. drjudithorloff.com/Free-Articles/The-Health-Benefits- of-Tears_copy.htm.

Palermo, Elizabeth. *Niels Bohr: Biography and Atomic Theory.* May 14, 2013. http://www.livescience.com/32016-niels-bohr-atomic- theory.html.

Planck, Max. *The Observer,* January 25, 1931.

Post, Huffington. *http://www.huffingtonpost.com/2013/11/21/us-life- expectancy-oecd_n_4317367.html.* November 21, 2013. http:// www.huffingtonpost.com/2013/11/21/us-life-expectancy- oecd_n_4317367.html.

Prolonged Grief Disorder: Psychometric Validation of Criteria Proposed for DSM-V and ICD-11. Holly G. Prigerson, et al. PLOS, December 17, 2013. http://dx.doi.org/10.1371/annotation/a1d91e0d-981f-4674-926c-0fbd2463b5ea.

Ross, Nancy Wilson. "The World of Zen: An East-West Anthology." 74. Vintage.

Roth, Mark. "After a death, some people go through prolonged suffering called complicated grief." *Pittsburgh Post-Gazette,* March 15, 2016.

Rouse, Margaret. "Quantum Theory." *What Is. com.* January 2015. http://whatis.techtarget.com/definition/quantum-theory.

Shear, Dr. Katherine M. The Center for Complicated Grief. https://complicatedgrief.columbia.edu/the-science-behind-our-work/cgt-research/.

Shear, Dr. Katherine M. *Complicated Grief Treatment- evidence-based treatment is available.* https://complicatedgrief.columbia.edu/complicated-grief/complicated-grief-treatment/.

Stephenson, John F. *Death, Grief and Mourning.* Simon and Schuster.

Strayed, Cheryl. *Brave Enough.* Alfred A. Knopf, 2015.

The Universality of the Golden Rule in World Religions. May 1, 2016. http://www.teachingvalues.com/goldenrule.html.

Waldman, Paul. "American War Dead, by the Numbers." *The American Prospect.* May 26, 2014. http://prospect.org/article/american-war-dead-numbers.

Waters, Owen. *Mysticism as a Key to Scientific Breakthroughs.* http://www.infinitebeing.com/0406/mysticscience.htm.

Williams, Lilee. "Doctors find this kind of grief is so severe, you can see it on an MRI." *Rare, Health and Medicine,* June 12, 2015.

Wilson, John. *The Nature of Complicated Grief.* January 17, 2014. http://johnwilsononline.org/2014/01/17/the-nature-of-complicated-grief/.

Zisook, Dr. Katherine Shear and Dr. Sidney. "Grief and bereavement, what psychiatrist need to know." *World Psychiatry,* 2009: 67-74.

About the Author

RHONDA O'NEILL IS a writer and blogger who shares the process she went through to heal from complicated grief after the deaths of her husband and son, who died within two years of each other. She is a registered nurse who worked in the specialty of pediatric intensive care. Currently, she volunteers her time working to prevent child abuse within her community as a member of the Wichita Coalition for Child Abuse Prevention.

A Kansas native, Rhonda is remarried and lives with her husband and twelve-year-old daughter in Wichita. You can follow her blog at www.theothersideofcomplicatedgrief.com. You can also follow her Twitter account, GriefSurvivor@GriefGirl2015. She has a community grief support page on Facebook: The Other Side of Complicated Grief. She is also a blogging contributor to the *Huffington Post*.

Made in the USA
San Bernardino, CA
06 December 2016